The Prostate

J. I. RODALE

RODALE BOOKS, INC.
Emmaus, Pa.

STANDARD BOOK NUMBER 87596-029-4

COPYRIGHT 1969 BY J. I. RODALE

ALL RIGHTS RESERVED

PRINTED IN UNITED STATES

E-900

FOURTH PRINTING — AUGUST 1969

*This work is dedicated to
the hundreds of thousands
of doctors who, if they but knew it,
could be and should be greatly interested.*

Contents

1. What Is a Prostate?

IF YOU HAVE ever had to drive for miles and miles while the need to urinate kept building up and no filling station (Perhaps it should be called an emptying station in this case.) in sight, then you know exactly where your bladder is. It is at that point in the lower abdominal cavity where you felt all that pressure.

Right at the central point where the pressure was most intense, is the exit of the bladder. It empties into a long, narrow tube called the urethra which carries urine out through the penis in a man.

It is through this same urethra that seminal fluid is ejaculated during sexual intercourse. Obviously, the sex glands must also be intimately connected with the urethra and must empty their secretions into it. That is why a malfunction of the prostate, which is a sex gland, is most frequently experienced as problems connected with urination.

Picture numerous bunches of grapes, with each stem joined to the stem of the adjacent bunch, and all of the principal stems connected to and emptying into the urethra at a point just below the exit of the bladder. The bunches of tiny bulbs that we have described as resembling bunches of grapes form a ring around the urethra and are contained within a sheath of muscle tissue. The entire sex gland that is called the prostate in a mature man is normally about the size of a walnut.

PHYSIOLOGY OF THE SEX GLANDS

Slightly above and behind the prostate, on either side of the urethra, there are two tiny sacs called the seminal vesicles. These are a storehouse for the sperm cells that are produced in the testicles. The fact that the sperms have to make their way up from the testicles to get into the seminal vesicles provides the guarantee that the sperms stored there will be alive and active.

And it is the secretions of the prostate gland that keep the sperms alive and active so that they can perform their sole task of fertilizing the female ovum. The seminal vesicles do not empty directly into the urethra, but rather into the prostate. What happens is that at the moment of orgasm, the muscle tissue surrounding these glands contracts. Sperm cells are forced into the prostate and mixed with prostatic fluid which is forced into the urethra and by a series of contractions ejaculated through the penis.

Herbert R. Kenyon, M. D., in his book "The Prostate Gland" (Random House, 1950) points out some of the nutrients that the prostate furnishes to the sperms. The basic composition is similar to that of the egg, being largely albumin which is the most complete and highest grade protein known, and lecithin, a compound of the essential fatty acids. In addition there is an enzyme called acid phosphatase that maintains a low acidity of the prostatic fluid. Other investigators have found substantial amounts of vitamins C and A, both of which are prime fighters against infection and toxicity. The minerals zinc and magnesium are also present in unusual concentration.

PROSTATIC FLUID NOURISHES SPERMS

Although much is known about the function of the prostate, and it can be said with assurance that this gland is vital to fertility in the male, our knowledge is by no means complete as yet. Dr. Kenyon along with many others believes that at least one hormone concerned with the general

health and functioning of the body is manufactured in this gland. So that even though it
is possible to lose one's prostate without loss of
potency, there is every reason to believe that
when this gland is removed, it is far more than
fertility that vanishes with it. Loss of the prostate
is a serious matter, even though there is little
reason to fear that the operation will be fatal.
Its removal can sometimes be necessary, but
should be thought of only as a last resort. Only
if the organ should actually be cancerous is
there any reason to hasten into surgery. As this
book will show, there have been numerous types
of bloodless and drugless treatments, all of
which have had some success in eliminating
prostatic difficulties. All of them seem to me
infinitely preferable to surgery, and in general,
I believe that surgery should not even be considered until less drastic methods have been
tried and found ineffective.

SURGERY IS
A LAST RESORT

This does not mean, however, that difficulties
with the prostate should be taken lightly, or
ignored in the hope that they will go away. Some
kind of remedial action is always indicated.
There is always the danger that the ailing prostate, even though it may be absolutely painless,
will enlarge and because of its anatomical
position circling the urethra, in enlarging con-

NOT TO BE
IGNORED

strict the urethra and impede or completely stop the passage of urine. Such a condition can be extremely painful and can become fatal if not treated.

Gray's Anatomy gives the following summary of dangers implicit in prostatitis: "*The prostate gland is occasionally the seat of suppuration (pus formation) either due to injury, gonorrhea, or tuberculous disease. The gland, being enveloped in a dense unyielding capsule, determines the course of the abscess and also explains the great pain which is present in the acute form of this disease. The abscess most frequently bursts into the urethra, the direction in which there is least resistance, but may occasionally burst into the rectum, or more rarely in the perineum. In advanced life the prostate becomes considerably enlarged, and projects into the bladder so as to impede the passage of the urine. According to Dr. Messer's researches, conducted at Greenwich Hospital, it would seem that such obstructions exist in 20 per cent of all men over 60 years of age. In some cases the enlargement affects principally the lateral lobes, which may undergo considerable enlargement without causing much inconvenience. In other cases it would seem that the middle lobe enlarges most, and even a small enlargement of*

DANGERS IN
PROSTATITIS

this lobe may act injuriously by forming a sort of valve over the urethral orifice, preventing the passage of the urine, and the more the patient strains, the more completely will it block the opening into the urethra. In consequence of the enlargement of the prostate a pouch is formed at the base of the bladder behind the projection, in which water collects and cannot entirely be expelled. It becomes decomposed and ammoniacal, and leads to crystitis."

URINARY RETENTION

There is no scientific agreement as yet as to just why the prostate becomes enlarged in later life. Dr. Kenyon states that "Practically all of the functional disturbances of the prostate gland result from its relationship to sexual activity." It is his opinion, in other words, that if early in life a man could arrive at a definition of what constitutes normal sex activity and live up to this definition, he could virtually assure himself against the later enlargement of the prostate (called hypertrophy) that plagues increasing numbers of men past the age of 50. On the other hand, Willard E. Goodwin and Donald C. Martin of the University of California's School of Medicine, in *Current Therapy* (1965) say that *"The clinical picture of chronic prostatitis is not infrequently a mild degree of the acute inflammatory condition. It may be associated with*

SEX ACTIVITY INVOLVED

chronic urinary tract infections or it may be the only manifestation of genitourinary disease." These authorities feel that the condition is more frequently a result of some type of infection than it is of sexual behavior, although they acknowledge that "it is sometimes associated with irregular sexual function and prolonged or recurrent sexual frustration."

A third point of view, and one that finds favor with many doctors, is concurred in by Robert M. Overton, a leading authority on the prostate of the chiropractic profession. He says "For many years the medics have propounded the fact that all men over 40 should expect prostatic trouble. It appears they are correct."

AGE

Yet as the following pages will show, there is very good reason to believe that in many cases the enlargement of the aging prostate gland and its attendant difficulties are basically a reflection of nutritional deficiency with any other causes only contributory and permitted to occur only because the nutritional deficiency exists in the first place.

NUTRITION IS BASIC

In any case, prostatic difficulties are no joke and must be taken seriously. And it is just plain foolish to wait until you have difficulties with your urination, which is a fairly advanced stage of the disease, before doing something about it.

Any of the following symptoms are an indication that it is time to visit your doctor for a check on the condition of your prostate.

(1) Low back pain.

(2) Blood in the urine or in the seminal fluid.

ATTEND TO PROBLEMS AT ONCE

(3) An increase in sexual excitability or frequent erections that come without any special stimulation.

(4) Pain during the ejaculation of the seminal fluid.

(5) Impotence or premature ejaculation.

(6) A chronic sense of fullness in the bowel and difficulty in defecation.

(7) Any decrease in control over urination, such as difficulty in starting or stopping the stream or inability to slow the stream.

When you consider that though it is not probable, it is at least possible that difficulties with the prostate might indicate an acute infection, an attack of tuberculosis, a venereal disease that you might not have known you had, or even cancer, it should be obvious that if you even suspect that there is anything wrong with your prostate, the first thing to do is get to a good doctor for an accurate diagnosis of just what the trouble is.

2. Surgery ?

O NE OF THE most common ailments that lead to surgery is prostatic disease. Men usually don't like to boast of it. If it is appendix trouble you may never hear the end of it, but when it involves the prostate it is usually kept *sub rosa*. So one does not realize how prevalent it is, and one knows very little about what it is. The patient is therefore unduly frightened when he hears that he needs prostatic surgery, and is usually glad to get it over with, not realizing that his trouble in many cases can be cured without an operation.

I have seen several men, who were slated for prostatic surgery, defeat the knife by adopting better nutritional habits and taking more exercise. I remember one case in which a man from Denver, Colorado, was in a hospital, to be operated for the removal of his prostate gland which was to take place the next morning. He had brought along some magazines, one of which was *Prevention,* in which there was an article on the prostate. After he read it he told the doctor that he had changed his mind, that he was going home, which he did. By applying what he had read in *Prevention* he soon got his prostate into pretty good shape. On a trip to New York, this man later on stopped off to see me and to thank me for having published the article that saved his prostate.

I thought you might be interested in the particular article. It was in the May, 1955, issue of *Prevention* and I reprint it herewith:

"Earlier articles mentioning the prostate gland and difficulties that may arise around it have brought in so many inquiries from *Prevention* readers that we did considerable research to uncover whatever else we could find that might be helpful for readers who want to avoid prostate gland trouble later on. We found precious little information. The prostate gland is removable. Because prostate trouble can be eliminated by an operation, little definitive research has apparently been done on what causes such

SURGERY
SUCCESSFULLY
DEFERRED

16

trouble and what, aside from an operation, can be done to help.

"If the prostate gland were not situated as it is, the enlargement that occurs so frequently in later years might go completely unnoticed. But this gland is located around the mouth of the bladder. So when it swells it cuts off the tube leading from the bladder and, since urine cannot flow freely as before, complications arise rapidly.

POSITION LEADS TO TROUBLE

"The prostate gland is an auxiliary sex gland, concerned with manufacturing the fluid in which the sperm cells float. Hence the removal of the gland usually results in sterility, even though generally it does not otherwise affect the sexual powers of the individual. In some cases it may. Until quite recently, removal of the prostate gland was a dangerous operation with a high mortality. In recent years less than 2% of patients die of prostate gland operations. The time in hospital has been cut to a minimum and, in general, members of the medical profession urge removal of the gland when it is causing difficulty.

SURGERY IS SELDOM FATAL

"Since disorders of the prostate occur mostly in the years past middle-age, it might seem likely that surgery mortality would be high because of the advanced age of the average patient. We have the word of John A. Taylor, M.D., of New York in the *Journal of the American Medical Association* for October 27, 1951, that prostatectomy (removal of the prostate gland) is not especially hazardous even for patients in their nineties. Since 1945, 41 operations have been done at St. Luke's Hospital on patients over eighty, and Dr. Taylor has performed 27 operations on his private patients over eighty. In one case the patient was 96 years old. Most of the patients had other diseases as well, the most common of these being hardening of the arteries and heart disease. There was a total mortality of 3.1% among these elderly patients which seems to indicate that the operation, as performed today, carries little risk.

AGE DOES NOT INCREASE RISK

"The decision to have an operation is generally the result of a lot of misery, for an enlarged prostate gland is both dangerous and painful. At first the only symptom may be a feeling of congestion and discomfort. Then there may be difficulty in starting the stream when urinating. There may be a feeling of fullness in the bladder, necessitating frequent trips to the bathroom, even though the amount of urine voided may be small. The residual urine--that remaining in the bladder--causes trouble. First there may be dribbling of urine. Then, as urination becomes more and more difficult, the contents of the bladder may accumulate to such an extent that they flood back into the kidneys, causing the very serious and immediate danger of uremic poisoning.

"It is assumed that any sensible person will have consulted a doctor long before this last stage is reached. Actually, however, he will soon discover that, aside from an operation, there is little or nothing the doctor can do for him to bring permanent relief. A catheter inserted into the bladder will drain off the accumulated urine, but shortly it will accumulate again. Massage of the prostate gland is often helpful in reducing its size. This must be done frequently. Hot baths may relieve congestion. Some physicians suggest hot sitz baths—that is, baths in which just the lower part of the trunk is immersed, while the chest and legs are not.

TREATMENTS OFFER ALLEVI-ATION ONLY

"What possible role does good nutrition play in preventing disorders of the prostate gland? The fat soluble vitamins seem to be most concerned with the health of this gland, just as they are with the well-being of cells and tissues throughout the lining of the digestive and reproductive tracts. We know that a lack of vitamin A has a very definite reaction on these tissues. One of the earliest symptoms of vitamin

VITAMIN A IS INVOLVED

A deficiency is a sloughing away of cells on the lining of the digestive, respiratory and reproductive tracts. Just as the tissues of nose and mouth may clearly indicate a vitamin A deficiency, so the delicate and sensitive tissues of the reproductive tract reflect any deficiency.

"We know, too, that vitamin E plays an important part in the health of the reproductive tract. Many experiments with animals have shown that a deficiency in vitamin E will create all kinds of problems in sexual life, for both the male and the female. In animal experiments these difficulties can be speedily corrected by giving vitamin E. This is one reason why good animal feeds always contain ample vitamin E.

VITAMIN E AND WHEAT GERM HORMONES

"Wheat germ oil, too, is noted for its effectiveness in preventing disorders of the sexual organs. It is given to both males and females in animal experiments and has proved itself of great value. It is believed that the natural hormones that occur in wheat germ oil are responsible for its powerful effect. It is made from the reproductive part of the wheat, of course, and carries with it all the substances that safeguard the reproductive processes of the grain.

"Another fat soluble vitamin, vitamin F (the unsaturated fatty acids) have been named by two researchers as curative of enlarged prostate gland. James Pirie Hart and William LeGrande Cooper, M.D., of Los Angeles, California, conducted an experiment involving nineteen patients to whom they gave unsaturated fatty acids. No other treatment was given. Writing about this experience in a pamphlet published by the Lee Foundation for Nutritional Research, 2023 W. Wisconsin Avenue, Milwaukee, Wisconsin, these investigators give their results as follows:

1. All cases showed a lessening of residual urine--that is, urine remaining trapped in the bladder. In 12 of the 19 cases there was no residual urine at the end of the treatment.

2. For 13 of the 19 patients, the treatments ended their getting up at night to urinate.

3. There was a decrease in fatigue and leg pains and an increase in sexual libido in all patients.

4. Cystitis or bladder inflammation cleared up as the residual urine disappeared.

5. Dribbling was eliminated in 18 of the 19 cases.

6. The force of the urinary stream was increased.

7. In all cases the size of the prostate gland was rapidly reduced.

"There are other physicians who are experi-

VITAMIN F
FOUND OF VALUE

menting with diet in relation to prostate gland disorders. We want to review in detail an article which appeared in the *American Journal of Digestive Diseases* for December, 1951. It is a preliminary report on a nutritional method for preventing surgery in cases of prostate enlargement. Benjamin F. Sieve, M.D., of Boston, who wrote it, had done considerable work along nutritional lines and has contributed many articles to scientific magazines. (We were informed that he is no longer living.)

BENJAMIN SIEVE, M.D.

"Dr. Sieve's theory in general is that vitamins and hormones (the substances produced by the body's glands) work together to create health. Infection, emotional upsets and mechanical interference with food intake prevent a proper nutritional state. In studying 200 cases, Dr. Sieve found that infection was one of the main causes of nutritional decline in 60% of the cases. Among men the most prevalent source of infection was the prostate gland. Along with the infection went nutritional deficiency and disorders of the glands and hormones. All three had to be cleared up in order to get the patient back into a healthy state.

INFECTION AND NUTRITION

"Dr. Sieve made a careful study of 100 patients who suffered from prostate trouble. The age range was from 15 to 75 years, with the majority in the 43-63 age group. In 70% of these the stage at which it would have been necessary to operate was prevented and no operation was necessary. Dr. Sieve's treatment, by his own admission, is purely preventive. He does not guarantee anything in the way of cures for patients with advanced cases. Instead he suggests that treatment should be started in the thirties, especially in those men who have a history of recurring infections. The younger the patient, the easier it is to correct his nutritional state, hence the infection, and hence the condition of the prostate.

PREVENTION STARTS YOUNG

"The first patient he describes was 20 years old and suffered from headaches, lack of appetite and pain in his legs. He also had acne, brittle, ridged fingernails, and other indications that all was not well nutritionally speaking. Dr. Sieve prescribed a full and well-balanced diet, along with vitamin supplements containing vitamins A, C, D and E and the vitamin B complex. In addition, he was given another preparation containing vitamin B.

"And, in case there might be difficulty assimilating these vitamins, vitamin injections were given once a week. The patient was also given by mouth and by injection various hormone substances that his condition indicated he needed. In addition a course of prostatic massage was given. Four years later the young man was quite well. He was still taking the vitamin preparations and Dr. Sieve said he hopes the youth realized their importance enough to go on taking them the rest of his life. He also stated that he could predict that this patient would never suffer from prostate enlargement, barring acute infection.

PROPER DIET AND MASSAGE FOUND BOTH THERAPEUTIC AND PREVENTIV

"The second case was 35 years old, a man who complained of fatigue and extreme sluggishness as well as distress in his digestive tract resulting in gas, vomiting and abdominal pain. There were many other symptoms indicating wrong diet for a period of years. And the prostate was "boggy." In addition to the vitamins A, B, C, D and E in large amounts, this patient was given a capsule containing the fat soluble chlorophyll substance from alfalfa, buckwheat and soybean (did this possibly contain the precious vitamin F?). Furthermore, he was given vitamin injections and gland medication. He had prostate massage once a week. And his prescribed diet was well balanced.

"Twelve months later he showed great improvement in many directions. He had not noticed any stomach distress for more than eight months. He had lost 12 1/2 pounds of excess weight. He had not been absent from work for a single day in seven months. The prostate gland was much smaller and no possibly dangerous nodules were to be found in it. For five years he continued to improve. Dr. Sieve comments that 'a good...clue to the type of case in which prolonged infection can be anticipated is for example the individual who gives a history of having had severe acne at puberty.'

SUBCLINICAL NUTRITIONAL DEFICIENCY

"He reminds us further that these cases of nutritional deficiency he is describing are not 'full blown, classic textbook cases,'...but the findings all add up to 'subclinical nutritional deficiency.' That means, just enough deficiency to bring about countless ills, such as acne, prostate enlargement, fatigue, headaches and so forth, but not enough deficiency to result in scurvy or pellagra or one of the other vitamin deficiency diseases. This is the condition we talk about so much in *Prevention*--this dragging, listless, tired state of health that most of us have, which could, with proper nutrition, be changed to vital, glowing health.

"The third patient Dr. Sieve treated was 55 and had been warned by a number of specialists that an operation on his prostate was absolutely necessary. His complaints were dribbling and frequent urination at night. He had also suffered an attack of coronary thrombosis. As Dr. Sieve examined him he noted many symptoms of vitamin deficiency (in nails, tongue, skin, etc.)

"His prescription was similar to those mentioned before--large doses and injections of all the vitamins and treatment for glands. The prostate was massaged once a week. Five months later the patient looked and sounded like a new man--free from headaches, no pain in his heart, slept better and had lost all symptoms of the prostate difficulty. At this time he was also given the tablets made from the soybeans, alfalfa and buckwheat...At eight months even greater improvement was shown and, says Dr. Sieve, the patient looked twenty years younger.

"You will notice that Dr. Sieve did not give his patients just one or two vitamins--they got them all, and in large quantity. And in addition to a good, well-balanced diet. By a good, well-balanced diet we mean a diet high in protein (meat, fish, eggs) with little or no food made from white sugar and white flour products, a diet that includes plenty of fresh fruits and vegetables and nothing that is refined, processed, degerminated or chemicalized. In addition, get your extra vitamins as Dr. Sieve's patients did: fish liver oils for vitamins A and D, brewer's yeast or desiccated liver for the B vitamins, rose hips for vitamin C and perhaps most important of all, wheat germ oil, vitamin E and the unsaturated fatty acids, otherwise known as vitamin F."

Another case was that of a personal friend of mine who also saved himself from a prostate operation by following the whole *Prevention* system. Here is another cure, described in a letter from a chiropractor, R.F.M., who writes us:

REPEATED SUCCESSES

"A recent issue of *Prevention* carried an article on the beneficial results of including vitamin F in the daily diet. I have had some trouble along that line with my prostate gland for the past few years, and various kinds of treatment have not proved successful.

"I sent for the brochure and read it carefully. The result they obtained with control groups, suffering with prostatic disorder, was almost amazing in its simplicity, and I decided to follow the method they used in the addition of vitamin F to my diet. My improvement was noticeable within five days. It was no longer necessary for me to go to the bathroom at night. The flow of urine was stronger, bladder pressure was relieved and dribbling ceased. I am including vitamin F in my diet, and intend to continue."

A reader who relieved a prostate condition by giving up a food to which he was apparently allergic is Mr. Jon Assenat of Charleroi, Penna. He writes, "I am nearing 70 and enjoying very good health. I was troubled with prostate one year, then I read in *Prevention* about cutting out orange juice. I had been taking it daily, but decided to stop. Since then I have never had trouble with getting up nights."

Prevention shuns citrus fruits because of their acid content, which is too strong an acid for the body to handle. It can lead to all kinds of trouble, but I never thought it could be responsible for a prostate condition. Still if its effect is to reduce the general health of the body, it might affect any gland or organ which happens to be in a weakened condition for some other reason.

ELIMINATION OF ORANGE JUICE

3. Diagnosis

I T HAS ALREADY been indicated that if you experience even slight difficulties in urination, or persistent low back pain or a sudden decrease or increase in your sexual desires, it is urgent that you have your doctor check on the condition of your prostate. If there is anything wrong with this gland at all, the probability is that it will be the so-called "benign prostatic hypertrophy" or gradual enlargement of the gland for no discernible reason. This is true of the majority of cases and does not call for emergency measures. If that is the diagnosis, you certainly have time to attempt to benefit the condition yourself before resorting to any more extreme measures.

MOST CASES
ARE BENIGN

There is enough possibility, however, that your symptoms may have been caused by some kind of condition requiring immediate medical attention, that it would be the height of folly to delay going to the doctor and at the very least insisting on a thorough examination and careful diagnosis.

There are, for example, numerous types of germ infection that are easily and quickly treated with antibiotics once the infecting germ has been identified. Dr. Von Luckum of the Mayo Clinic, writing in that organization's periodic reports a few years ago, identified the predominant infection that clinic had found in cases of prostatitis as being *streptococcus*. *Staphylococcus* ran it a close second. Many cases are due to infection from an old and supposedly cured case of gonorrhea and some may be due to the vaginal infections to which some women are prone, notably *trichomonas vaginalis* and *candida albicans*.

INFECTIONS ARE EASILY TREATED

There are cases in which an infection of the kidneys or the bladder will pass into the prostate and by causing prostatic symptoms, provide the first opportunity to discover that these serious infections exist. The most frequent such infection is tuberculosis of the kidneys. Rectal infections can also pass into the prostate and troubles can be caused by kidney or bladder stones. And it should never be forgotten that the prostate is one of the sites in which cancer is prone to develop.

If you have any of these conditions, you want to know about it and you want to have it treated as fast and as thoroughly as possible.

For most of the germ infections, which are most frequently involved when it is not simple benign enlargement of the gland, there are specific antibiotics that will effectively and expeditiously eliminate the infections once they are identified. As a general thing, I do not approve of antibiotics. I believe the body's natural resistance to infection is far more important and more to be relied upon. I disapprove strongly of the heedless rapidity with which doctors will dispense these potent drugs with all too potent side effects, without even bothering to determine first whether they are necessary. But it is not to be denied that when an accurate diagnosis has found them necessary, antibiotics perform an enormously valuable and quite desirable function.

ANTIBIOTICS SERVE AN IMPORTANT PURPOSE

Even though I prefer to do without antibiotics in general, if I had an infection in my prostate gland I'd be very glad to have my doctor eliminate it in 48 hours, and I'd rely on the generally high level of my nutrition to help me fight off the side effects.

Unfortunately, an examination of the prostate and of areas that might be causing possible prostatic complications is neither simple nor comfortable. For the sake of accurate diagnosis, however, it is better to put up with the discomfort and even to insist on a thorough examination in case the doctor is a little bit lazy about it.

EXAMINATION IS UNCOMFORTABLE BUT NECESSARY

The first step in such an examination is usually a probing of the prostate area with a finger inserted up the rectum. This is the simplest and most direct avenue of approach and in many cases will enable the doctor to determine an existing enlargement, whether or not there is an abscess, and even when there is a possibility of cancer. For each of these conditions, the entire gland usually will present a distinct texture to the educated finger that knows what it is looking for. A great deal can sometimes be learned by such a simple probing.

In addition, the doctor may very well perform what is usually misnamed a "prostate massage" and is actually the application of a light pressure in the proper direction to strip the gland, which is to say, to force its contents into the urethra. This causes a discharge from the penis which

PROSTATE MASSAGE

can then be examined in the laboratory for possible infectious organisms.

There is also a nasty little instrument known as a cystoscope which a doctor can insert into the urethral canal through the penis and right into the bladder, where a light and a series of reflecting mirrors enable him to look directly into the bladder and determine whether a cyst has been formed because of residual urine or for other reasons. To make a complete determination of the size and shape of the prostate, the doctor will have to take an x-ray, which again is a nasty process because it is hard to get an x-ray picture of glandular tissue. What he has to do is pump air into the bladder which then makes it possible to see the prostate as a shadow outlined against the light bubble picture of the air-inflated bladder.

INTERNAL INVESTIGATION

Such an examination is nothing to look forward to, obviously. Yet it is far more reassuring in the long run to be told there is nothing fundamentally wrong after an examination of this type, than to have to suspect that the doctor is just guessing.

BETTER TO KNOW

"Every patient in whom prostatic obstruction is discovered does not require operative intervention," says Dr. Herbert R. Kenyon in his book *The Prostate.* This, of course, is true. But while we have seen that there are many ways to bring relief to those with enlarged prostates where the situation is not a medical emergency, Dr. Kenyon, like most doctors who have an insufficient knowledge of what can be accomplished nutritionally, seems to feel that short of surgery, catheterization is the only way to bring symptomatic relief to the man with an enlarged prostate. Catheterization is an unpleasant but sometimes necessary technique of draining a bladder that is otherwise too obstructed to void urine. This is accomplished by insertion of a soft rubber or plastic tube through the urethra into the bladder. Depending on what is considered the best solution to the individual problem, the catheter can either be immediately removed, once the bladder has been drained, or more commonly it is left in place for several days or even longer, keeping the bladder empty while the results of other treatments are studied and it is determined whether the size of the prostate has been reduced to a point that will permit normal urination again.

DRAINAGE OF BLADDER BY CATHETER

Of both methods Dr. Kenyon says that, "Catheterization, either intermittent or indwelling, involves the risk of carrying bacteria into a previously uninfected bladder and of causing irritation and infection of the urethra itself.

INFECTION IS A RISK

These complications can be prevented or minimized by careful aseptic precautions and the concomitant administration of suitable drugs or antibiotics possessing the power to combat such developments. There is also a possibility that a catheter, lying in the urethra, will cause infection of the epididymis (a small body lying just above the testicles) testicles or both."

And he then goes on to say that before catheterization, he recommends a minor operation to tie off the ducts leading from the testicles to the seminal vesicles to reduce the danger of infection.

All in all, it can be seen that catheterization is a cumbersome, painful and sometimes dangerous process which still, in itself, can only provide temporary relief and never cures anything. It is no wonder that if prostatic enlargement has reached a point of making catheterization necessary, most doctors will prefer to operate on the gland, removing it either completely or partially and making certain of bringing long-term relief.

CATHETER RELIEF IS ONLY TEMPORARY

Surgery on the prostate has now become what is considered a minor operation in that, except where cancer is involved, there is just about no chance of dying of it. As has been pointed out in other portions of this book, however, the prostate, like most other glands, is still largely a mystery. Its complete function is not known. Neither is its complete nature or the complete structure of its complex secretions. Nobody really understands just what the relation is between the prostate gland and general health, vigor and youthfulness, but there is certainly a relationship. To a surgeon, removing a gland that is causing discomfort and may cause complications can seem a quick and easy answer. Personally, I would not remove anything--not even a fingernail--until I was convinced there was absolutely no other solution. Removing a prostate gland will not destroy sexual abilities and while it will probably sterilize a man, that is no great problem to the man of middle age or older. Nevertheless, I'd rather keep mine and I'm sure you would rather keep yours.

UNNECESSARY REMOVAL IS FOOLISH

4. The Pumpkin Seed

IN 1958 THERE BEGAN a pleasant correspondence between Dr. W. Devrient of Berlin, Germany, and myself. Somehow he obtained possession of a copy of *Prevention,* and was attracted by its naturalistic approach to disease prevention. He was curing patients of prostatic trouble by having them eat pumpkin seeds and felt that we should know about it. He had written an article on the subject in the magazine *Heilkunde Heilwege* (January, 1959), and I am presenting a translation of it here:

Institutes of Biological Healing Methods
Berlin

In almost all men of 50 years of age and upward, deviations in normal urination can be observed: a man who formerly slept through the night, now must wake up once or twice (or even oftener) to urinate. The person concerned has now come near to the difficulties that are related to the gradual weakening of function of the genitourinary canal and particularly to changes in the prostate gland as caused by age. These involve enlargement of the gland (adenoma of the prostate gland, generally referred to as prostatic hypertrophy) that plays such an important role in the normal hormone production of the masculine body. At the age of 50 and over, more than 60% of all men have this trouble, over 60 this increases to 80%. Prostatic hypertrophy may be regarded as a sign of the steady pursuing of the aim of Nature: through such enlargement a functionally weakened organ seeks to make up for the cessation of hormonal vigor. However, this is only partially successful: the hormonal balance remains disturbed, the masculine part is on the decline, the feminine continues growing disproportionately. Because of this hypertrophy, discharge from the bladder is interfered with. There sets in a disposition to disorder, which one does not admit, although potency too generally begins to slacken. If this first stage of hypertrophy is neglected, in its later development is involved pronounced

AGE BRINGS
WEAKENING
OF FUNCTION

HORMONE
BALANCE
DISTURBED

disease of the prostate gland, the second and third stage of which constitute a real scourge of men in general and more and more often in our times lead to surgical operations with protracted hospital confinement. This disease (prostatic adenoma) was formerly less common, but today as the cause of death for men of 65 it amounts to about one-third. Its presence can be demonstrated in every fourth American once he has reached the age of 52. It is maintained that the number of impotent males in the USA amounts to some two million. This too is related to the hormone production of the prostate, although all these processes are centrally regulated. In Berlin two large specializing urological hospitals had to be founded, because the surgical divisions of the existing hospitals were not sufficient. The causes of this trouble are to be sought in false methods of living. The poisoning of the glands with tobacco plays the most important role among them.

TWO MILLION
IMPOTENT MEN

TOBACCO
POISONS
THE GLANDS

"Foresight is better than rueful hindsight," says the wise proverb. Unfortunately, it fails to specify preventive measures in the way of preservation of the glands. Doctors, therefore, are intent on pointing out the necessity for early diagnosis, so that through prompt intervention hypertrophy is prevented and retention of urine with its dread consequences prohibited. This is of momentous importance, because through stoppage of urine, when hypertrophy is advanced, severe bladder and kidney damage can result (uremia). Treatment with synthetic hormones favors the evolution of cancer rather than prevents it. We biological physicians therefore reject this treatment, basing our opinion on the conviction that an artificial hormone, though chemically identical, still does not for long have the same effect as a natural one.

RETENTION LEADS TO UREMIA

In view of the fact that, with the exception of operative urology (highly dangerous prostatectomy) and biophysical therapy, modern medicine has not been able to find any successful weapon against early attrition and deterioration of the prostate gland, we have no other recourse than to seek prevention in the realm of healing plants. The lore of medicinal plants knows in effect of the influences of drugs which prevent the abovementioned symptoms of early stages of hypertrophy. There is in fact a till-now little noticed, disease-preventive plant whose rejuvenating powers for men are extolled with praise by popular medicine both in America and in Europe. Experience reveals that men in those countries where the seeds of this plant are copiously eaten throughout a lifetime remain completely free of

MEDICINAL PLANTS A BETTER WAY

prostatic hypertrophy and all its consequences.

The above mentioned neglected curative plant contains active biocatalytic (reaction-causing) ingredients which I should like to call "androgen-hormonal." These biocatalytic ingredients are building-stones for the development of male hormones. Their presence brings about the synthesis of the hormones and also their all-important equilibrium. This is particularly important because it is precisely these male hormones of the prostate that slacken in productivity with increasing age. Therein originates a disturbance of hormonal equilibrium and consequently the attempt (condemned to failure) of the body to work out an adjustment on the way to compensatory hypertrophy. From this benign adenoma later there frequently develops the disposition to cancer.

HORMONAL EQUILIBRIUM

After this introduction it is now time to reveal the secret and to mention the name of the plant and why I call it "neglected." When readers learn that the plant is the well-known pumpkin (*Cucurbita Pepo*), some of them will possibly be disappointed and wonder why the pumpkin is called "neglected."

NEGLECTED PUMPKIN

To that it should be answered that the pumpkin, in relation to its nutritive value, is very seldom offered for sale and consumed. However, we should not at this point occupy ourselves with the nutritive-physiological importance of the pumpkin, but with the important pharmacological properties of its seeds, the constituent ingredients of which are far from having been investigated.

Therapists are primarily interested not in the chemical composition, but in the effect. Pharmacognosy draws upon the drugs of popular medicine, tests them and then passes them on to doctors, who, to begin with, are content with the knowledge that the drug is harmless and has been successfully tested by popular medicine. Then begins its use and investigation in practice and clinic.

Now we arrive at the explanation of why the pumpkin can be considered as a neglected plant. From the appended summaries of the literature (for which I am beholden to those great connoisseurs of plant medicine, K. W. Thiele, of Ennepetal-Ruggeberg in Westphalia, and Dr. W. Winkelmann, of Lustmuhle, St. Gallen, Switzerland) one can note that there is repeated mention of pumpkin seeds as a vermifuge (to expel worms) but only in 2 cases is their efficacy as a medication in the preventive treatment of prostatic hypertrophy spoken of. Herein, however, is the main point of the theme of this

VALUE FOR PROSTATE LARGELY UNKNOWN

publication. So long as the pumpkin was found interesting only as a nutritional factor in animal fodder and its seeds only randomly used as a gentle vermifuge, the most important recommendation of this precious plant--and its relations to the genitourinary tract--remained as good as unknown to pharmacology and clinical medicine. Hugo Schulz, the eminent pharmacologist, mentions pumpkin seeds in only 3 lines of his "Lectures on the Effects and Usage of German Medical Plants" (*Vorlesungen uber Wirkung und deutschen Arzneipflanzen, Leipzig, 1929*). Only the plain people knew of the open secret of pumpkin seeds, a secret which was handed down from father to son for countless generations without any ado. No matter whether it was the Hungarian gypsy, the mountain-dwelling Bulgarian, the Anatolian Turk, the Ukrainian or the Transylvanian German--they all knew that pumpkin seeds preserve the prostate gland and thereby also male potency. In these countries people eat pumpkin seeds the way they eat sunflower seeds in Russia: as an inexhaustible source of vigor offered by Nature.

AN ESTABLISHED FOLK REMEDY

Investigations by Dr. G. Klein at the Vienna University revealed the noteworthy fact that in Transylvania prostatic hypertrophy is almost unknown. Painstaking researches resulted in the disclosure that the people there have a special liking for pumpkin seeds. A physician from the Szekler group in the Transylvanian mountains confirmed this connection as an ancient healing method among the people. Dr. Bela Pater, of Klausenburg, later published these associations and his own experiences in the journal "Healing and Seasoning-Plants" (*Heil-und Gewurzpflanzen,* 12, 18, 1929).

EATERS AVOID PROSTATE TROUBLE

My assertion of the androgen-hormonal influence of pumpkin seeds is based on the positive judgment of old-time doctors, but also no less on my own personal observations throughout the years. This plant has scientifically determined effects on intermediary metabolism and diuresis (excessive urination), but these latter are of secondary importance in relation to its regenerative, invigorative and vitalizing influences. There is involved herein a native plant hormone, which affects our own hormone production in part by substitution, in part by direct proliferation (production of new growth). Anyone who has studied this influence among peasant peoples, has been again and again astonished over the effect of this plant in putting off the advent of old age. My own personal observations in the course of the last 8 years, however, have been decisive for me. At my own

PLANT HORMOI VITALIZES

age of 70 years I am well able to be satisfied with the condition of my own prostate, on the basis of daily ingestion of pumpkin seeds, and with that of my health in general. This beneficial result can also be found among city patients who are prudent enough to eat pumpkin seeds every day and throughout their life. But one must continue proving this to the city-dweller. The peasants of the Balkans and of Eastern Europe knew of the healing effect of these seeds already from their forefathers.

PROVED
ON SELF

The centuries-old experiences of popular medicine reaching Western Europe gradually not only from Eastern Europe, but also from Central-America, where the pumpkin is said to be indigenous, induced science and industry to extensive researches. A great quantity of substances have been discovered, but it cannot be said to which of these substances the specific effects are related. Industry has manufactured suitable preparations in which the pumpkin seed comprises a component ingredient in the form of an extract. Such preparations have been proven effective in the hands of doctors, on precise prescription, in the realm of general treatment. What Western Europe is in urgent need of, however, is the possibility of providing the world of ailing men as generously with

SUPPLY OF
SEEDS NEEDED

pumpkin seeds as in the case in Eastern Europe, the Balkans and the Near East. The surest road to this is the supplying of good pumpkin seeds in dried and hulled form.

After painstaking study I came to the realization that the pumpkin seed is able (1) to cure the first stage of prostatic hypertrophy (excessive growth) and (2) to improve the second stage by converting it back to the first stage, to say nothing of its preventive influence that is factually attested. Its manner of influence is so profound that a subjective improvement can often be observed even in the third stage. Thus, it can be made completely believable that active ingredients are present in the pumpkin seed that are able to eliminate the primary condition of swelling of the prostate and to the extent even that a favorable preventive influence can be exerted on cancerous degeneration.

PROFOUND INFLUENCE IS EXERTED

Once these indications were firmly established, I was on the lookout for places where these precious pumpkin seeds could be procured both for my patients and for myself. Apothecaries, drug-stores and health-food stores had hardly any demand at all for this article and were at a loss as to where to direct me. Mr. J. G. Fink of Sindelfingen, the expert planter and worthy pioneer of linseed, saved me by showing me the way out. He supplied me every year with from 8 to 10 kilograms (1 kilogram equals 2.205 pounds) of choice pumpkin seeds for my personal use. Similarly, he also supplied those of my patients who shared my opinion that nothing was too expensive and no effort too great to preserve the prostate gland.

I hope that the pumpkin will never again be referred to as a neglected plant. Nature grows a plant to combat every disease, and to fight off the dread "male disease" she offers us the pumpkin seed.

I published Dr. Devrient's letter, without any comment, in *Prevention,* the magazine for health. A number of my readers were sufficiently intrigued to give pumpkin seeds a try, and see if their prostate conditions could be helped.

After a few months, and somewhat to my own surprise, we began getting dozens of letters from men telling us how supposedly hopeless prostate conditions had been helped by pumpkin seeds. In time I received more than a hundred such letters. Below are reproduced a few that I consider most typical. It is not considered very scientific to publish testimonials, and I probably would not do it if any of our scientific researchers had ever taken pumpkin seeds

READERS
WERE HELPED

seriously enough to make clinical trials of their effects on the prostate. But there are no such clinical trials.

The only evidence I have of the effectiveness of pumpkin (and also sunflower) seeds is Dr. Devrient's letter and the letters of more than a hundred grateful readers who tell me that they personally have been helped. That is enough to make it seem that pumpkin seeds might very well help at least certain individuals among the millions of present and future sufferers from prostatic hypertrophy. It seems to me that it would be a shame to suppress such information just because nobody has bothered to test it under controlled experimental conditions.

UNPROVED, BUT WHY NOT TRY IT?

I do not say it is proven, but I do say that this information might be of help to you and I know you will be interested in it. Here, then, are testimonial letters I have received that are typical in every way of those that readers keep sending me regarding pumpkin seeds and their prostate trouble.

I am a man who will be 82 the 22nd. of April, 1964. An article in the *Prevention* magazine of September had a section that was about the prostate gland trouble that pumpkin seeds and sunflower seeds would help. I got some and I

DISTURBED NIGHTS

want to tell you that they sure helped me. I was getting up to urinate 5, 6 and 7 times a night and in two weeks after I started taking the seeds I was about all over my troubles and now I only get up one or two times a night.

M. F. TAYLOR
Leadore, Ohio

I am a subscriber to *Prevention* magazine. I am 65 years old. After reading two articles relative to the subject on the prostate, I began taking pumpkin seeds in September 1963. At that time, I had to see a specialist as I was having trouble in passing and visiting the bathroom at night too many times.

RETENTION
IMPROVED

After taking the seeds for six months, I can report a positive improvement. I can now pass without any difficulty. I also pass 50 per cent less during the day and visit the bathroom only once each night, and many nights, not at all. I expect to use the seeds the rest of my life and feel confident that an operation will never be necessary, because the seeds positively have retarded the growth of the prostate.

Thanking you again, I am gratefully yours,

JACK EILENBERG
Brookline, Mass.

P.S. I neglected to state that I had blood staining when I began taking the seeds. About 6 weeks ago the staining stopped and has not recurred.

My painful prostate condition has entirely gone since pumpkin seeds and sunflower seeds have been powdered in our blender to make a breakfast food that is delicious.

ARTHUR WELLCOME

Waltham, Mass.

I want to congratulate you on the articles which you have been having for the last few months in *Prevention* on the prostate. I have been suffering from prostate trouble for a considerable number of years and all the average doctor seems to know about it is to tell you it is holding its own or you have to have surgery sooner or later. I have even been told by one of the top urologists in New York City, that he has never heard of any of the things that you mentioned in your articles.

NOT HELPED BY DOCTORS

I have been taking vitamin F and eating a lot of pumpkin seeds and am much better for it; for all of which I am very grateful to you.

CARL HOLMES

New York, N. Y.

In an attempt to find out why pumpkin seeds might be of such value, I have had several chemical analyses made of them. They were

ZINC AND FATTY ACIDS

found to be extremely rich in the trace mineral, zinc (from 40 to 50 parts per million) and in linoleic and oleic acid (vitamin F) which comprised 37 per cent of the total content of the pumpkin seed. When you read the chapters on vitamin F and zinc, you will understand the possible significance of these elements.

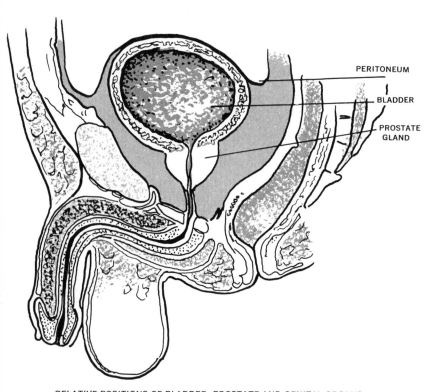

PERITONEUM

BLADDER

PROSTATE GLAND

RELATIVE POSITIONS OF BLADDER, PROSTATE AND GENITAL ORGANS

5. Magnesium

T HERE IS A REMARKABLE book published in French, called *Equilibre Mineral et Sante*, Mineral Equilibrium and Health, by Dr. Joseph Favier (*Librairie le Francois*, Paris), and while the title indicates that it deals with minerals, the actual fact is that it deals mainly and specifically with the mineral magnesium... the miracle mineral. The book shows how valuable magnesium as a medicament is for many diseases, but its chapter on magnesium's effect on the prostate should be discussed in this symposium on the prostate. Unfortunately for those who would like to read it, it is out of print.

DR. JOSEPH
FAVIER

Dr. Favier gives a Dr. Stora credit for being the first to discover magnesium chloride as an effective agent in treating urinary troubles of prostatic origin. He informed the Medical Academy of France of it, on March 18, 1930. Eight days later, Dr. Pierre Delbet submitted a report showing the same results with magnesium chloride.

When Dr. Stora spoke about his results to Favier, the author of the book we are discussing, Favier began to make inquiries among his physician friends. He found that they were all taking magnesium chloride. To his surprise he found that four out of five of them had been disturbed by difficulties in urinating, especially at night. And all of them, after taking the magnesium tablets, found that their nocturnal urinating troubles diminished or disappeared.

Another doctor--Chevassu--gave him other interesting data about 12 prostatic cases whom he treated with magnesium tablets. Ten of them were cured. One disappeared, and he does not know what the result was with him. The one that was not cured was left with nothing more than nightly urination. The interesting thing is that the general physical condition of all these patients improved. Evidently, there is something about magnesium that is healthful for the body.

Dr. Chevassu speaks of his Case No. 4, a 77-year-old prostatic patient who suffered a crisis of complete retention of urine. He had to be probed in order to urinate. His prostate was very much enlarged. Probes were carried on three times a day up to November 24, and hot clysters (enemas) were administered. The first spontaneous urinating took place on November 25; the probes were cut off on December 7. On December 10, the patient urinated five times a night and he had a big residue.

The magnesium treatment started on December 14, the dosage being 4 tablets (2g.40), and went on until February 21, 1930. The nightly urinatings fell from five to three, and the residue dropped to 20 grams.

NIGHT RISINGS REDUCED

The patient, having recovered his strength and feeling very well, believing he was cured, discontinued the treatment. Urinating's frequency increased and three days later on February 24, the residue had gone up to 126 grams. The magnesium treatment was resumed, the urinating's frequency curtailed and on March 21, the patient informed the doctor that he urinates only two to three times per night.

Regarding patient 13, who had been a case of complete retention of urine: he was sent to the hospital in order to have an operation of the prostate performed; that is, to have his prostate removed. But Dr. Chevassu felt that the operation in his case would be too dangerous. He was therefore given the magnesium chloride tablets. Spontaneous urination occurred, and the patient left the hospital without the operation. From then on he had no difficulty or pain with his urinations. Thereafter the patient used to come to the hospital regularly merely as a friendly visitor to show his gratitude to the doctor. He was, of course, taking magnesium tablets after he left the hospital.

SPONTANEOUS URINATION BROUGHT ABOUT

Doctor Favier ends the chapter by saying that among the men who have been taking magnesium chloride tablets for many years, none to his knowledge has suffered from prostatic trouble.

In connection with some of these cases and their cure, Dr. Pierre Delbet in the verbatim record, *Academy of Medicine* (Paris), session of March 25, 1930, says, in regard to how magnesium acts on the body:

"As magnesium adds to the contractibility of smooth muscle fibers, one may wonder if the treatment doesn't act uniquely on the bladder, inasmuch as there isn't any parallel between reduction in the size of the adenoma (a tumor of glandular origin) and functional improvement. But if, in certain cases, this improvement is considerable, when reduction in size is slight,

MODE OF ACTION

which is favorable to the hypothesis, in other cases, it's quite the contrary, the reduction is quite more marked than functional improvement.

"In an earlier communication, M. Bretau and I have shown that age is accompanied by a reduction in magnesium in the most active organs and that the absorption of halogenated salts permits a struggle against certain manifestations of senility.

AGE BRINGS MAGNESIUM DEFICIENCY

"Hypertrophy of the prostate is a complaint of waning life and perhaps the one which strikes most terribly. The facts communicated by M. Stora, which I have just reported and which belong to M. Chevassu, show that it is one illness which can be modified by halogenated magnesium salts.

"The preceding observations show that halogenated magnesium salts sometimes have an extraordinary action in very advanced cases. The sick man in observation 13, who had complete retention, comes to see me regularly at Cochin to express his gratitude. He came right at the time of my retirement, that is to say during 16 months. He continued to take the treatment and urinated without difficulty.

TREATMENT CONTINUOUS

"Since that time, a number of prostate sufferers, whom I don't know, have expressed their gratitude to me for the services that delbiase (a magnesium compound) rendered them.

"Its mode of action is completely obscure to me. What is striking is that the effects stop from the moment that the treatment is stopped. The subject of observation (4) is an example. His nocturnal urinations were reduced to three and the residue, which had been considerable, fell to 20 grams. He stopped the treatment, and, in three days, the frequency of his urinations increased and the residue rose to 125 grams.

"One of my former pupils, a distinguished surgeon, has communicated his own observation to me. It appears to be very interesting. He had nocturnal urinations whose frequency increased all the time. He put himself on the delbiase regimen. His urinations became less frequent. 'My life,' he said, 'was completely untroubled. I could only complain that urinations were a little more frequent and a little more demanding than I should have liked.' At the beginning of the war, he was mobilized and sent to be a surgeon at the front, where he couldn't get any delbiase. His urinations became more frequent and assumed painful proportions. His general health was affected. Two and a half months after the treatment was stopped, it was noted that he had a residue of 220 grams.

"In sum, the effect of halogenated salts of

MAGNESIUM MUST NOT BE STOPPED

magnesium isn't lasting. They improve or even suppress functional difficulties; they don't heal the lesions. They cause them to retrocede in a certain number of cases, but they don't cure them. As soon as the treatment is stopped, the development begins anew. Doesn't that prove in a peremptory manner that an insufficiency of magnesium in the organism is the cause, or at least one of the causes, of these lesions?"

I would like to discuss some of Delbet's ideas on senility. He says that all organs and tissues do not age at the same speed. The muscular system generally lasts the shortest period, the nervous system the longest. "The role of magnesium in organic synthesis leads one to think that it must diminish with age. Weiske's work shows that magnesium is less abundant in the bones of old rabbits than it is in those of young ones." In the human testicles a decline in magnesium was demonstrated as a person ages, but in old age calcium is more abundant than magnesium--three times more abundant. But here is something extremely interesting. As Dr. Delbet puts it, calcium is considered as a "framework" mineral, but magnesium is an "action" mineral. Calcium is static, magnesium is dynamic.

TESTICLES DEVELOP DEFICIENCY

He says, "Added calcium and diminished magnesium are the characteristics of the senile testicle. In the brain and in the testicle, the relationship of magnesium and calcium and the modifications of the relationship with age are of the same degree, but it appears certain to us that at the time that life is waning, magnesium diminishes, while calcium rises. Now, everything that is known about the chemical activity of magnesium, about its powers of synthesis of organic magnesium compounds, about its action in the synthesis of chlorophyll, justifies one in thinking that its reduction plays a role in senility, or at least in certain phenomena of senility."

RELATED TO SENILITY

Now, if magnesium in the body becomes less abundant as we grow old, and since medical researches prove that deficiencies of magnesium lead to many diseases, isn't it common sense to take magnesium as a food supplement on a permanent basis?

As Pierre Delbet says in his book, *The Prevention of Cancer,* "Salts of magnesium are not medicaments. They are necessary food." But I would rather take the milder form of magnesium, namely dolomite tablets, rather than the more soluble magnesium salts.

FOOD, NOT MEDICINE

Regarding Delbet's statement that added calcium, and diminished magnesium are the characteristics of the senile testicle, I would not reduce one's daily intake of bone meal! I would rather eliminate completely all milk, butter and cheese products which deplete the system of magnesium. We must have a fair amount of calcium. We can't eliminate it!

At this point I would like to discuss another physician's experience with a magnesium drug, which I read about in 1952, in *The Archives of Pediatrics* for July of that year, entitled "Light Magnesium Carbonate in the Treatment of Acute Glomerular Nephritis," by C.L. Thenebe, M.D., of West Hartford, Connecticut.

It seems that the usual practice in treating this form of kidney trouble is to use magnesium sulphate...which, by another name, is known as epsom salts. The sulphates to my knowledge are bad actors and are implicated in the causation of cancer. Dr. Thenebe found magnesium sulphate to be nauseating to his kidney patients, so he changed over to magnesium carbonate. In magnesium carbonate, the latter fraction is quite innocuous. In fact on the average, about 40 per cent of the contents of plants are made up of carbon. Dr. Thenebe used the magnesium carbonate on eight patients, and said: "Comparably, magnesium carbonate tastes much better (than magnesium sulphate) and is not at all nauseating. It is harmless in large doses." He obtained

C.L. THENEBE, M.D.

MAGNESIUM
CARBONATE

his magnesium carbonate from the Merck Drug Company.

What I would like to suggest is that since magnesium carbonate is much safer than the magnesium chloride we have been discussing under Dr. Favier's account of the treatment of the prostate, that it be tried instead of the magnesium chloride. Perhaps in emergency cases the treatment can start with the chloride form, and change over to the carbonate when the condition has alleviated itself.

Now it is important for all men approaching the dangerous age as far as the prostate is concerned, namely, about 40, to try to get a diet rich in magnesium. Dolomite is the richest source I know of magnesium carbonate. Bone meal is very rich in this element. Three-fourths of the body's magnesium, whether in man or animal, is in the bones! Wheat germ is also extremely rich in it, as well as honey and kohlrabi. Other foods that have goodly amounts of magnesium are: almonds, dried lima beans, beet greens, brazil nuts, cashew nuts, corn, endive, hazelnuts, peanuts, dried peas, pecans, brown rice, soy flour and walnuts. As far as pumpkin seeds are concerned--they are especially rich in this important mineral element. So are sunflower seeds.

DOLOMITE RICH IN MAGNESIUM CARBONATE

There should be a strong accent on a sufficiency of magnesium in the diet to protect the body against many diseases. There is much research evidence available on this subject, yet the medical profession rarely stresses the value of magnesium in the diet.

Although knowledge of the essentiality of magnesium is comparatively new, it has been known since about 1930. In 1932 Dr. Schrumpf-Pierron, Professor of Medicine at The Sorbonne in Paris, studied the health of 13,000,000 Egyptians to conclude that magnesium in the diet plays a vital role in the prevention of cancer.

He found that wherever people ate food deficient in magnesium, the cancer rate was significantly higher. After his monumental paper was published, the investigation was repeated and checked in France by Dr. Pierre Delbet of the French Academy of Medicine. After exhaustive soil and crop analyses and statistical studies, in 1944 he published *Politique preventive du cancer,* confirming completely the Schrumpf-Pierron discovery that magnesium is a cancer preventive.

In the U.S., there is widespread magnesium deficiency in the states of New Jersey, Maryland, Virginia, both Carolinas, Georgia and Florida, and there is some lack in Illinois, Michigan,

MAGNESIUM AND CANCER

New York and the New England States. With our nationwide distribution of food, we can never tell when we might be getting what we eat from one of these low-magnesium regions.

Why take chances? Bone meal, pumpkin seeds, and the other foods I have mentioned will protect you.

PROTECTIVE FOODS

Here are a few of the many letters I have received from men whose prostate problems have been helped by magnesium in the form of dolomite.

I have had prostate trouble for over 20 years. I had all the standard treatments but none helped; only temporary.

Then on the First of March, 1964, I was operated on for an obstruction at the neck of the bladder and knots on the prostate gland. It helped a lot to relieve the pressure on my bladder. I still had a high pus count in my urine, also in my prostatic fluid. I went to the doctor every other week for a massage of the prostate to keep down the pus count. I still had bad lower back pain. I went to a chiropractor every day for 2 weeks then 3 times a week for a month but still had backache.

SUFFERED FOR 20 YEARS

I had taken some small pills that cost almost 50 cents each--4 per day--for 2 or 3 years.

When I received your magazine and read your article on magnesium and the prostate I started to take dolomite tablets--9 per day. After about 4 weeks, no more massages. My pus count dropped from 40 to 8. I took no other drug. To me that is worth crowing about and one of the best parts is that my backache has gone. I don't get up at night any more. I am 55 years old.

BACKACHE GONE

JAMES L. CREEKBAUM
Indianapolis, Indiana

About a year ago I realized that my trips to the bathroom were becoming very annoying and alarming. I began to fear prostate gland trouble. Then, I read your articles in *Prevention* on pumpkin seeds and dolomite tablets to control the prostate gland, so, now after taking four dolomite tablets and a handful of pumpkin seeds, every day, my condition has returned to normal, with no more rising during the night to the bathroom.

NIGHT RISING ENDED

JOHN J. COMFORT
Lansdale, Pa.

I have read your articles on magnesium dolomite and have had extra good results. Had acidity and canker sores under my dental plates, and tear ducts that were running all the time. I'm okay on these three troubles now. I also

OPERATION AVOIDED

cured myself of prostate trouble for which I was
about to have an operation.

ROGER CLARK

Beulah, Michigan

6. Vitamin F

V ITAMIN F is an important factor in the treatment of prostatic trouble. It is the general name of the unsaturated fatty acids. One of its best sources is lecithin. Fats are carried by lecithin, which dissolves easily in body fluids. In other words, the polyunsaturated fats in lecithin cause a homogenization of the cholesterol portion of fat and prevent its accumulation on the walls of the blood vessels. My favorite food, eggs, is very rich in lecithin, and should be part of everyone's diet, including heart cases ...the only contra-indication being certain surgical cases. Seeds are also very rich in vitamin F.

Vitamin F has been named by 2 researchers as curative of enlarged prostate gland. James Pirie Hart and William LeGrande Cooper, M.D., of Los Angeles, California, conducted an experiment involving nineteen patients to whom they gave unsaturated fatty acids. No other treatment was given.

STUDY OF 19 CASES

Hart and Cooper began with a careful examination of their 19 cases. Not only were detailed case histories recorded, but the size and degree of the enlargement of the prostate gland was determined and a thorough physical examination of each established that there were no other vitamin, mineral or hormone deficiencies that could be blamed for the abnormal condition of the prostate. The patients were then placed on a daily dosage of six 5 grain tablets containing a concentrate of linoleic, linolenic and arachidonic acids. The linoleic and linolenic acids are considered the most potent of the unsaturated fatty acids and the ones that are best utilized by the body. Arachidonic acid is the form into which the others are converted by body chemistry before it does its vital work within our systems. This dosage, which is very high, was administered for three days which was enough to saturate the systems of the patients. Then it was reduced from six to four tablets

UNSATURATED FATTY ACIDS

daily, and several weeks later reduced to one or two tablets.

These investigators give their results as follows:

(1) All cases showed a lessening of residual urine--that is, urine remaining trapped in the bladder. In 12 of the 19 cases there was no residual urine at the end of the treatment.

UNIFORM IMPROVEMENT

(2) For 13 of the 19 patients, the treatments ended their getting up at night to urinate.

(3) There was a decrease in fatigue and leg pains and an increase in sexual libido in all patients.

(4) Cystitis or bladder inflammation cleared up as the residual urine disappeared.

(5) Dribbling was eliminated in 18 of the 19 cases.

(6) The force of the urinary stream was increased.

(7) In all cases the size of the prostate gland was rapidly reduced.

HYPERTROPHY REDUCED IN ALL

Although they themselves used purified concentrates, because that is the only way to get controlled results that are acceptable as scientific evidence, Hart and Cooper point out in their report that the purer forms of unsaturated fatty acids do not exhibit as much vitamin F effect as natural oils, which are high in these acids. That is why, instead of recommending such purified concentrates, I prefer to recommend lecithin as a source of vitamin F.

The word comes from the Greek *Likithos,* meaning the yolk of an egg. For lecithin is most abundant in egg yolk. In fact, when it was first studied in Germany towards the end of the last century, the researchers could then obtain lecithin only from egg yolk. What is this lecithin? It is a fatty emulsion of several of the valuable unsaturated fatty acids, as they occur naturally in foods. It frequently occurs in conjunction with cholesterol, and other natural fat that requires lecithin for its proper processing and utilization by the system. It is only when food processing discards the lecithin from a fat source and leaves the cholesterol, that cholesterol in the diet becomes a danger.

As a source of lecithin, eggs are far too expensive. Not that you can't afford to eat the two eggs a day that I recommend, but if you wanted to go to your health food store and buy lecithin extracted from eggs, you would find that very costly indeed. That is why lecithin was not widely used or known until a cheaper source was found.

Today, lecithin for human consumption is made chiefly from soybeans. In fact, soya-lecithin

LECITHIN

has come to be the name generally used for lecithin because it is practically always made from soybeans. The way soya-lecithin was discovered is typical of our modern blundering way of doing things. Soybeans have become a profitable crop in this country and the oil they contain is used for all kinds of different products, most of them having nothing to do with food--rubber, petroleum, paint, ink, leather, soap, shaving creams, putty and so forth. So, as the chemists were devising ways and means of using this perfectly splendid food to manufacture these various non-food articles, they found that one substance interfered with many of the processes they wanted to use. So they removed the substance--lecithin. It became a waste product.

DERIVED FROM SOYBEANS

REMOVED FROM OIL

Isn't that a typical feat of modern genius--to remove from a good product the main substance that makes it valuable as food and then sit and ponder what to do with it so it won't be wasted! Lecithin is used in some food processing for it is a good emulsifier outside the body as well as inside. But it apparently never occurred to anyone that it was put into soybeans for some nutritional purpose, and certainly it would never occur to anybody to put it *back* into foods so that they would be more nourishing! In our country today the food industry seems bent on making food just something that will last a long time on grocery shelves, will look pretty and will be convenient. And of course all of this means that more and more nutritional value must be sacrificed.

Here is a letter, but the name has been lost:

"Proper foods are essential, and the elimination of certain foods are equally as essential. I can eliminate my lecithin complex for 30 to 60 days, and eat hominy grits for 4 or 5 days and my prostate gland trouble will come back on me and will take 2 to 3 weeks to get back natural."

Here are some foods rich in lecithin and vitamin F:

Liver	Pumpkin Seeds	FOODS RICH IN VITAMIN F
Brains	Beef	
Wheat Germ	Barley Seeds	
Safflower Oil	Corn Seeds	
Corn Oil	Sunflower Seeds	
Soybean Oil	Nuts	
Melonseeds	And Eggs	

Don't overlook eggs...2 eggs daily to help preserve the health of the prostate.

It is also desirable to take at least one lecithin capsule at each meal.

I would like to quote some material about lecithin from a Rodale Press book, "The Complete Book of Food and Nutrition":

"So here we have disorders as widely varied as hardening of the arteries, acne, diabetes and psoriasis benefiting from the administration of lecithin. And we have a perfectly sound reason for why these diseases should be increasing daily. Look at the menu the next time you are in a restaurant. A goodly portion of the main dishes are fried in deep fat or prepared with fat. This means prepared with hydrogenated shortening from which the lecithin and vitamins have been removed. Dessert consists of a variety of pastries, pies and cakes, all made with hydrogenated shortening or synthetic fats which also contain no lecithin. Salad dressing is made from refined oil--again no lecithin. Margarine is probably used on vegetables or bread. Margarine goes through a dozen or so processes at high heat, guaranteeing that no vitamins or lecithin will remain in it. In addition, your restaurant meal has included 'hidden' fats--the cracker with your tomato juice probably contains synthetic shortening--the bread probably does, too.

HYDROGENATED FATS CONTAIN NO LECITHIN

"So almost everything you eat in a restaurant today brings into your body cholesterol without bringing along with it the lecithin that is necessary to emulsify it and keep it from collecting in lethal amounts on the walls of blood vessels. Is it any wonder that hardening of the arteries kills, either directly or indirectly, more Americans than any other disease?

"At home what do you eat? If you use hydrogenated shortenings (that is, the white, solid shortening like Crisco) for any purpose whatsoever, you are inviting disaster. If you use either margarine or butter, if you use crackers or any other prepared foods made with shortening, if you buy baker's bread, or, in fact, anything from a commercial bakery, chances are you are getting, every day, large amounts of cholesterol and no lecithin to help your body manage the cholesterol properly.

CHOLESTEROL

"What is left for you to eat in the way of fats? Only completely natural fats that have not been tampered with in any way. This is a difficult assignment, for you have been used to buying all kinds of things you believed more wholesome which you can now no longer buy. Egg yolks are still probably the best food you can eat from the point of view of lecithin content. Although poultry raisers have invented a lot of incredible things to do to the chickens that lay eggs, they have fortunately not as yet discovered any way they can get inside an eggshell and do things to the egg before it reaches you. You will get cholesterol in your egg yolk, yes. But you will also get the lecithin that belongs with it, so the

EGGS ARE
VALUABLE

yolk can't do you any harm."

In their report of the treatment of prostatic hypertrophy with vitamin F, Hart and Cooper are able to state by way of conclusion that "every patient exhibited enthusiasm over the improvement in physical well-being resulting from treatment."

I am throwing in a letter from R. D. Reusch of Berkeley, California, which deals with parsley and the prostate:

"A year ago I met a doctor who took a trip to the Netherlands. There he discovered what the people use for all urinary tract troubles. Would you believe it? It is the lowly plant called parsley taken two or three times a day, steeped as tea, quite strong. The doctor came back and started to recommend it to his patients.

RELIEF FROM PARSLEY

"Ever since I started to take parsley I got relief, both from bladder irritation and prostate pressure. Now after over a year I feel so grateful I want to pass it on to others that suffer as I did."

7. Amino Acids

A SUCCESSFUL NON-SURGICAL treatment for enlarged prostate gland is cause for rejoicing among the thousands of mature men who yearly face the possibility of becoming victims of this painful and dangerous affliction. Such a treatment has been discovered by Doctors Henry Feinblatt and Julian Gant and is reported in the *Journal of the Maine Medical Association* (March, 1958). Of almost equal importance is the fact that the medication used is not a drug to dull the pain or mask other symptoms, but a nutrient which exists naturally in food and attacks the problem at its source, curing completely in many cases. Its effectiveness in treating prostatitis was discovered quite

NON-SURGICAL
TREATMENT

by accident, but this fortunate accident can result in relief and cure for thousands of men whose only other recourse might have been an operation.

The prostate gland is located near the mouth of the male bladder. The gland itself functions as an auxiliary sex gland. It manufactures the liquid which acts as a vehicle for the sperm cells of the male. Without this important fluid there is no way of keeping the sperm alive long enough for transfer into the female vagina for the purpose of fertilizing the female egg, and hence in nearly every case there is no way of carrying out the normal process of reproduction. Without the prostate gland to manufacture this essential fluid, the male becomes sterile.

FERTILITY
REQUIRES
PROSTATE

In the early stages, the symptoms of enlarged prostate are rather vague--a feeling of congestion and discomfort in the pubic area. There follows a constant feeling of fullness of the bladder, with frequent, urgent trips to the bathroom. Once there, however, there is often difficulty in starting a stream, and sometimes no urination at all. The recurring need to void during the night is also common. Eventually, a residue of urine that has not been expelled is collected in the bladder and dribbling occurs. This is the unconscious release of urine, in small

DRIBBLING

amounts, forced out by a full bladder. When the urethra is interfered with to the extent that very little or no urine can escape from the bladder, the serious problem of possible uremic poisoning arises. This can occur when such large amounts of fluid accumulate that the bladder can hold no more. With the normal avenue of release through the urethra shut off, the urine floods back into the kidneys, presenting a grave danger of poison to the system.

UREMIC POISONING

A word should be said here about cancer of the prostate. For some unknown reason this gland is extremely susceptible to malignancy. When prostatic difficulties do occur it is wise, therefore, to make certain through a medical examination by your doctor that no cancer is present, before embarking on a system of self-cure. Sometimes surgery is the only recourse in such cases.

SUSCEPTIBLE TO CANCER

If the prostate swelling is simply a benign condition of enlargement, then the findings of Doctors Feinblatt and Gant, mentioned above, should be of great interest and help. As we said, the discovery of this treatment was a happy accident. It happened this way: Dr. Gant and a colleague were treating a group of allergic patients with a mixture of three amino acids (components of protein) -- glycine, alanine and glutamic acid. One of the patients thus treated volunteered the information that his urinary symptoms had disappeared while he took the amino acid mixture. This led to a trial of the same compound on non-allergic patients with urinary symptoms. Patients with enlarged prostates and associated urinary symptoms experienced prompt and rather spectacular relief. They remained free of the symptoms while taking the compound, but soon after discontinuing the medication, they had their symptoms once more.

GLYCINE, ALANINE, GLUTAMIC ACID

A controlled experiment was set up. A series of forty cases of prostatic enlargement, previously ascertained to be benign, or non-cancerous, were included. Symptoms of discomfort were present in 35 of the patients; 39 complained of the urge to void often during the night; 23 experienced delayed urination; 29 suffered with excessive frequency of urination; and 27 complained of extreme urgency to void which felt uncontrollable. The age range was 37 to 75 years. The average duration of their complaints was 4 years.

40 CASES

The forty men were divided into two groups. The odd-numbered cases were given glycine-alanine-glutamic acid in dosages of 2 capsules after each meal for two weeks. Then one capsule after each meal for three months thereafter. The second group, or even-numbered patients, were also given capsules on the same schedule, except that their capsules did not contain the amino acids, nor any other active ingredient.

Of the men who were treated with the amino acids, 92% saw the size of the swollen prostate diminish, and in 32% it shrank to normal size. The need to get up during the night to void unusually often was relieved in 95% of cases and completely eliminated in 72%. Urgent urination was relieved in 81% of the cases, frequency of urination was lowered in 73%, discomfort was lessened in 71% and delayed urination was remedied in 70% of the patients. There was no comparable improvement in any of the patients who did not receive the amino acids until, after two months, they were switched from the inactive capsules to the amino acid compound.

MORE THAN 90% RELIEVED

It would be hard to over-estimate the importance of this study by Feinblatt and Gant. More than 50% of all men past the age of 50 and 75% of those past 80 suffer from prostatic difficulties. Enlargement of the prostate, in itself, is considered of little importance. But when it causes urinary retention, something must be done about it. And the only effective permanent relief that medical science has known how to give, up to now, has been surgical removal of the prostate.

In such a situation, you would think that thousands of doctors would seize eagerly on a new treatment that gives promise of being easier, less expensive, and incomparably less dangerous. But the fact is that prostate removals continue to be performed with ever-increasing frequency, and hardly any doctors have taken the trouble to find out for themselves whether the Feinblatt-Gant treatment might not turn out to be easier and better.

SURGERY
FAVORED
BY DOCTORS

The Feinblatt-Gant discovery, after all, was accidental and involved a limited number of patients. The study was too small to lead to any broad, positive conclusions. But it should have stimulated an enormous amount of medical research, checking on their methods and their results and leading to conclusions that would have the firmest scientific foundation.

Instead, the study has been generally ignored. And surgeons keep working overtime developing slick new techniques for removing harmless organs in operations that might be proved to be unnecessary, if their profession would only take the trouble to investigate and find out.

STUDY IGNORED

One investigation that has been made was reported by Dr. Frederic Damrau of New York City in the *Journal of the American Geriatrics*

Society for May, 1962. Dr. Damrau was intrigued with the Feinblatt and Gant report and tried the same treatment on his own private patients. When he had prescribed amino acid therapy for 45 patients, using 40 others as controls who received placebos but no actual medication, he analyzed his results.

DR. DAMRAU CONFIRMED RESULTS

He found that amino acid therapy definitely worked on a large number of patients.

Fifty-six per cent of the patients receiving amino acid therapy were completely or partially relieved of the need to get up during the night to urinate, and forty-two per cent were completely relieved of this symptom. This compares with only fifteen per cent of the control group, who were relieved to some extent by the element of faith healing that always seems to have some effect when placebos are administered. Sixty-six per cent of Dr. Damrau's patients secured complete or partial relief of urinary urgency, with forty-two per cent — almost two-thirds of them — showing complete relief. Forty-six per cent of his patients were relieved of difficulty in maintaining a stream of urine, half of them completely relieved, while none in the control group showed any relief whatsoever of this symptom.

SUCCEEDS WITH MANY

"The results of a controlled study of 45 cases of uncomplicated benign prostatic hypertrophy,"

Dr. Damrau concluded, "have confirmed the findings of Feinblatt and Gant on the value of a glycine, alanine and glutamic acid combination as palliative treatment. After three months of medication, there was a significant reduction of the symptoms attributable to residual urine.... NO SIDE EFFECTS Statistically, the degree of relief was far greater than in the control group of 40 patients who took placebo capsules according to the identical schedule and for the same period of time. No side-effects were observed."

This is a highly important corroborative study. How much impression has it made on the medical profession? Well, ask your doctor if he has ever heard of either study. But he has heard how your prostate can be removed by freezing it, or chopping it into little pieces.

If you are suffering with this prostatic enlargement, perhaps you should call these studies to your doctor's attention.

There were no ill effects whatsoever in any of the patients as a result of the amino acid therapy. It was also noticed that edema, or swelling, EDEMA ALSO REDUCED of other parts of the body disappeared during treatment. Edema is known to be one of the most important symptoms of protein (source of amino acids) deficiency. Edema is also the result of too much salt, which retains water in the tissues.

It follows then that a diet low in salt and high in protein would be an excellent protection against the problems presented by a swollen prostate gland.

Foods Rich in These Amino Acids
(per 100 grams)

FOOD	ALANINE (Grams)	GLYCINE (Grams)	GLUTAMIC ACID (Grams)
Brewer's yeast	3.456	6.334	2.427
Milk, non-fat, dry	1.228	8.320	.703
Casein (milk protein)	3.354	23.052	1.987
Eggs	——	1.583	.543
Egg yolks	——	1.951	.571
Beef, lean. . . . . ·	1.086	2.846	1.164
Lamb, lean.	.955	2.594	.999
Veal, lean.	1.169	3.073	.942
Chicken	——	2.309	1.378
Fish—haddock	——	2.318	1.005
Liver, beef	1.261	2.679	1.198
Liver, calves'	1.216	2.584	1.155
Liver, chicken	1.414	3.006	1.344
Beans, kidney.	1.316	3.696	.392
Lentils	.888	3.700	1.080
Peanuts	1.094	5.932	1.710
Soybeans	1.571	7.010	1.595
Filberts.	——	3.079	1.421
Cottonseed flour and meal	2.155	9.122	2.322
Corn.	.995	1.765	.399
Whole wheat flour·	.465	4.156	.812

8. Zinc

P ROBABLY THE MOST neglected field in nutritional research is the study of the trace minerals and the many roles that they play in the functioning of our bodies. When it comes to the prostate, one of the trace minerals that we áre certain plays an important part in the health of this gland is zinc. Yet no one has ever succeeded in describing just what it is that zinc does in the prostate; and to tell the truth, there are very few that have made any attempt to find out how zinc functions in the prostate. We know that it must have an important function, however, because large amounts of zinc are stored in the prostate and there is an established relationship between disease of the prostate and deficiency of this trace mineral.

T. A. Mawson and M. I. Fisher, two scientists of Canada's Chalk River Atomic Project, made an exhaustive study of healthy and cancerous prostate glands, both in humans and in animals, to determine the difference in their mineral content. Reporting their results in the *Canadian Journal of Medical Sciences,* Volume 30, pages 336 to 9, they found that zinc is stored in very high quantity in the healthy prostate gland and in the sperm-nourishing seminal fluid secreted by the prostate. More zinc, they found, goes into the prostate gland than into any other human tissue. More important, "There was evidence of a decreased zinc content in glands containing malignant tissue." These two Canadian scientists did not pursue their work far enough to look for reasons, but they were convinced there was a definite connection between the amount of zinc in the system and the health of the prostate.

ZINC CONCENTRATE IN PROSTATE

It has been found that the semen itself is extremely rich in zinc. Three researchers, George R. Prout, M. D., Michael Sierp, M. D., and Willet F. Whitmore, M. D., who performed experiments with radioactive zinc and wrote about them in the *Journal of the American Medical*

Association for April 11, 1959, conclude their article on zinc and the prostate with this paragraph: "Sperm are richer in zinc than any human tissue studied, yet the testis is relatively poor in this element. From this observation alone, it would seem that zinc is related to spermatic physiology. It is conceivable that the prostate acts as nothing more than a purveyor and receptacle for zinc until ejaculation occurs and at this time zinc is incorporated in the sperm in a perhaps essential capacity. Certainly, under the conditions of the experiments, the unfailing appearance of Zn 65 (that is, radioactive zinc) in prostatic fluid and the prostate suggests that prostatic fluid without zinc would no longer be prostatic fluid."

SPERM RICH IN ZINC TOO

"There is no explanation for the high zinc concentrations found in the male mammarian genital tract, particularly in animal and human semen as well as in the epididymis and prostate," said Jean Mayer, Ph.D., associate professor of nutrition at the Harvard University School of Public Health, in *Postgraduate Medicine* (February, 1964). But then Dr. Mayer goes on in the same article to point out some facts about zinc that make it even more obvious what a vital role zinc must play, even if the few scientists who have shown any interest are still unable to

NEEDED BY SEX ORGANS

explain it. Studies cited by Dr. Mayer show that in the Near East, where zinc deficiency is widespread in certain regions, it leads to failure of the sex organs to develop properly. Describing such a group near Cairo, Egypt, Dr. Mayer states: "...their external genitalia were remarkably small, with both atrophic testes and small penises; and they had no facial, pubic or axillary hair....The diet of these subjects consisted of wheat or corn bread, beans, occasionally white cheese, and only rarely meat or animal protein other than cheese."

ATROPHY OF TESTES

Although apparently there was no examination of the internal sex organs, we can certainly guess that if these had been examined, they would have shown similar abnormalities of development.

In other words, to pin it down to the prostate, though it is not known how zinc maintains prostate health, it is known that a deficiency of zinc will lead to unhealthy changes in the size and structure of the prostate.

It is not unlikely that when the mechanism of zinc action is discovered, it will be found that what the zinc does in our system is to trigger the action of one or more enzymes that we must have working within us to maintain healthy prostate glands. An enzyme is a chemical fer-

ENZYMES INVOLVED

ment that we manufacture within our bodies. There are hundreds of enzymes, each with its own specific purpose although most of them are still relatively unknown. We manufacture enzymes to bring about every chemical change that takes place within our bodies, and other enzymes to stop these changes when they should be stopped. Our enzyme balance is enormously complicated and equally important. And there are at least a dozen enzymes that require zinc to activate them.

ZINC IS A CATALYST

Does the prostate synthesize some enzyme or group of enzymes, requiring activation by zinc, that makes it impossible to maintain a healthy prostate gland when there is a zinc deficiency? The answer to that question is not yet known. But it certainly does not seem unlikely.

Another fascinating possibility is raised by the recent discovery, reported by Drs. Sullivan and Lankford in the *American Journal of Clinical Nutrition* (Volume 10, February, 1962) that drinking alcoholic beverages increases the excretion of zinc and chronic alcoholics show a deficiency of this trace mineral. Is it possible that there is a relationship between drinking and subsequent prostate trouble?

ALCOHOL CAUSES DEFICIENCY

One of the biggest names in nutrition, Dr. Andre Voisin of *L'Ecole Nationale Veterinaire d'*

Alfort (Paris) in his book, "Soil, Grass and Cancer," (Philosophical Press) has an entire chapter called "Zinc and Premature Aging of the Tissues of the Prostate Gland." He draws attention to researches performed at the Winnipeg Hospital, reported in *Cancer,* Vol. 9, pages 721-726 (1956) where the zinc content of the prostate was studied as a function of its physiological state.

DEFICIENCY RELATED TO CANCER

Where there was a 35% drop in zinc from what is considered normal, a mild hypertrophy (enlargement in size) of the prostate gland was observed. Where there was about a 38% drop in zinc, it led to chronic prostatitis. But where the zinc dropped by two-thirds, it developed into cancer.

Voisin, who is an agricultural scientist, believes that part of the deficiency of zinc in the modern diet is due to the fact that modern farming methods with their use of artifical fertilizers and poisonous insecticides has caused a reduction of the amount of zinc in our food plants, which deficiency transmits itself to the cattle (meat) which man is consuming.

LACKING IN MODERN FOOD

Zinc is a trace mineral, that is, a mineral which is needed in miniscule, almost microscopic amounts by the human organism, and if not present, can lead to serious disturbances in he functioning of the body's organs and glands. n laboratory experiments, it has been found that a diet lacking in zinc can cause a decrease in growth of experimental animals, hair that does not grow properly, spots around the mouth, and changes in the eyes that suggest vitamin B deficiency. In the complete absence of zinc, reproduction is seriously affected.

It is important, therefore, that in our diet is included the zinc-rich foods. These are: brewer's yeast, onions, rice bran, eggs, nuts, molasses, rabbit, chicken, peas, beans, lentils, wheat germ, wheat bran, oysters, beef liver and gelatin. Most of the men with prostate involvements are suffering from a too refined, factory-food diet,... sandwiches, pies, and such.

ZINC-RICH FOODS

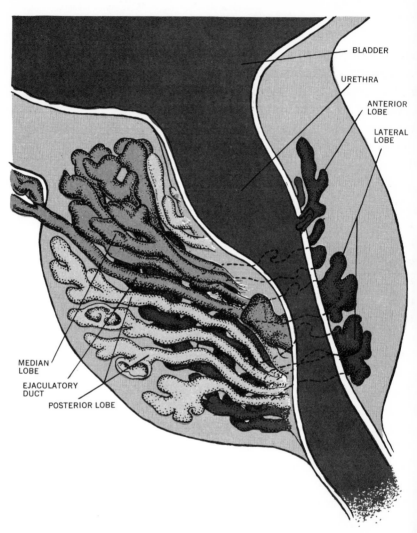

BLADDER

URETHRA

ANTERIOR
LOBE

LATERAL
LOBE

MEDIAN
LOBE

EJACULATORY
DUCT

POSTERIOR LOBE

HOW THE PROSTATE EMPTIES INTO THE URETHRA

9. Seeds, A Nutritional Miracle

I F THERE CAN BE SAID to be such a thing as a philosophy of nutrition, its first principle is surely that the seed must be the most complete food known. Perhaps, instead of seed, we should say seed foods. For in thinking about such foods, we include eggs--the seed of birds--among those foods that Nature has made miraculously rich in nutritive values. Milk might very well have the same status if man, with his pasteurization and chemical feeding, had not tampered with it to the point of making it a food unfit for human consumption. The crimes that have been committed against milk have made it a monstrosity rather than a miracle; but eggs and seeds remain natural foods that are whole in the truest sense of the word.

It is obvious why the seed must be a great food. It is the only food received by a new life and it must contain every element, bar none, that the new life requires to grow and mature. In addition, the fertile seed or egg contains the mysterious principle of life itself.

But what has this to do with the prostate? Everything. Although not everybody realizes this, the most basic drive of life in every living thing is reproduction. We know of many plants-- all the annuals--that die once they have accomplished their reason for being, which is to produce seeds. Animal and human mothers automatically rob their own bodies of the nutritive elements needed to create a new life, even if such robbery sickens or kills them. So we can be sure that in Nature's primal urge to reproduce, the seed foods that nourish the embryo, above all else, will contain the elements necessary for a healthy reproductive system.

LIFE ELEMENTS
IN SEEDS

Since the prostate gland is one of the essential links in man's reproductive system, this in itself is good reason to suppose that seed foods would be a valuable source of prostate health.

But what does human knowledge say about it? Does the analytical chemist confirm what philosophy leads us to suppose?

The answer is a resounding yes.

We have already considered a number of nutrients that have been shown scientifically to be of value in reducing prostate enlargement and alleviating or eliminating the symptoms of this difficulty. These elements are the three amino acids, glycine, alanine, and glutamic acid; zinc; magnesium; and the polyunsaturated fatty acids. These nutrients are the scientific key to the European belief we have reported as to the value of pumpkin seeds for prostatic health that does not diminish with age. The pumpkin seed, on laboratory analysis, is rich in every single one of the valuable health-building nutrients we have explored. The same seems to be true of all seeds, but they naturally vary from one variety to another. For the health of the prostate, the best foods would seem to be seed foods, and the best of the seed foods are pumpkin seeds, sunflower seeds, wheat germ and eggs.

Let us begin with the unsaturated fatty acids--vitamin F. It has already been pointed out that eggs are an extremely rich source of this vitamin, but how about the plant seeds? Because official food analysis tables seldom provide you with exactly the information you want, we had samples of pumpkin seed, sunflower seed and wheat germ analyzed by a Philadelphia labora-

WHAT SEEDS
CONTAIN

tory that is one of the largest and most reliable in the Eastern United States. It was found that the sunflower seed is richest of the three in linoleic acid, the most complete polyunsaturated fatty acid and the one from which the body can make the fullest supply of arachidonic acid, the form in which the human system utilizes vitamin F. Sunflower seeds, whether hulled or in the shell, contained 30 grams of linoleic acid per 100 grams of weight. Pumpkin seeds contained 20 grams per 100 grams, and wheat germ contained five. When we consider that even the five grams of wheat germ is a rich supply of this precious vitamin to be found in 100 grams of any food, then it can be appreciated how extremely rich in linoleic acid are both sunflower and pumpkin seeds.

RICH IN UNSATURATED FATTY ACIDS

Next in importance to linoleic acid as a polyunsaturate is oleic acid, and in this the pumpkin seed is richer than the sunflower. There are seventeen grams per 100 grams of weight of oleic acid in pumpkin seed, nine in sunflower seed, and three in wheat germ. Again it should be noted that even the three makes wheat germ a rich source.

Other seed foods rich in vitamin F are soybeans, watermelon seed, sesame seed, and all the nuts that are commonly eaten. It is apparent that if you make a habit of eating a good variety of seed foods and eating them every day, your prostate is bound to benefit by a rich supply of the essential unsaturated fatty acids.

We have already found that two of the trace minerals--magnesium and zinc--are of tremendous importance for a healthy prostate, and that prostate trouble may well be a deficiency in one or both of these minerals.

In magnesium, the egg falls down as compared with plant seeds. Agriculture Handbook No. 8, *Composition of Foods*, lists the magnesium content of whole eggs as 11 milligrams per 100 grams of egg. This may be enough for the reproductive system of a rooster, but it is not enough to do a human being much good so far as magnesium goes. Certainly it does not compare with wheat germ, which offers 336 milligrams of magnesium per 100 grams, or with sunflower and pumpkin seeds, each of which contain slightly more magnesium than wheat germ does--approximately 350 milligrams for the same quantity of seeds. It is calculated that the average diet in the United States is deficient in magnesium by about 200 milligrams a day. This alone could account for the increasing prevalence of prostate trouble. And isn't it remarkable that simply by eating 100 grams a day (about 3-1/2 ounces)

MAGNESIUM
DEFICIENCY

of either wheat germ, sunflower seed or pumpkin seed, or a combination of all three, the daily deficiency in magnesium consumption can be completely eliminated? Is it any wonder that in Russia and Eastern Europe, where everybody eats these seeds the way Americans smoke cigarettes, prostate trouble is practically unheard of?

Almonds, Brazil nuts, peanuts and other common table nuts are also splendid sources of magnesium as well as the polyunsaturated fatty acids.

NUTS CONTAIN MAGNESIUM

It is when it comes to zinc, though, that our chosen seeds leap ahead of all others as a source of substantial amounts--substantial that is for a trace mineral. For zinc is one of those metals that easily could be dangerous if we ate too much of it, yet is absolutely essential in small quantities. We would not recommend herring as a source of zinc. Its content of at least 70 and perhaps as much as 120 milligrams of zinc per 100 grams seems to us a dangerously large amount of a mineral we should be obtaining only in traces. Far closer to what we should get for prostate health is the 5.5 milligrams per 100 grams that are supplied by eggs, or the range between 4 and 6 milligrams per 100 grams that we find in pumpkin seed, sunflower seed and

ZINC CAN BE OVERDONE

wheat germ. For zinc, this is a substantial amount. It is far more than you'll obtain from any other nuts or seeds. There is indeed a biochemical distribution of elements in these particular seeds that makes it seem as if they were specifically designed to keep the prostates of men healthy.

It is only when we come to the amino acids glycine, alanine and glutamic acid, that we find that none of our chosen plant seeds is a complete source. If you eat some of each every day-- let us say, two eggs, an ounce of wheat germ, and an ounce or two each of pumpkin and sunflower seeds--you will get each of these three amino acids that have been shown to have a beneficial effect on the prostate. But no one of them will supply all three. For a good food source of all three, you could not do better than to also include some soybeans in your daily diet or to take a supplement of brewer's yeast, which of all known foods, contains the best balanced distribution in rich supply of all three of these amino acids. And eggs come close to brewer's yeast in this value.

Perhaps the best answer of all is not to concentrate on any one seed--not even the miraculous pumpkin seed--but to make certain that your diet contains every single day a variety

AMINO ACID DISTRIBUTION

of seed foods in substantial amounts. That is not only of the greatest benefit to health, but is also the pleasantest eating and the most fun.

10. Coffee and Sugar

A CCORDING TO THE STATISTICS of the Metropolitan Life Insurance Company, some 20,000 men in the United States die every year of prostatic difficulties (*Statistical Bulletin,* December, 1964). Fifteen thousand of these men die of cancer of the prostate; and the other five thousand of the effects of being unable to pass urine which is caused by the so-called "benign hypertrophy" of this gland.

20,000 DEATHS EVERY YEAR

In spite of this fantastically high rate of mortality connected with one small accessory sex gland, it is not the highest rate in the world. Sweden, Denmark, Norway, Switzerland and Austria all have more prostate-related deaths per 100,000 than even the United States.

At the other end of the scale, there is one country with accurately reported health and mortality statistics whose death rate for prostatic causes is almost unbelievably lower than that of any other. That country is Japan, where cancer of the prostate is almost unknown and even benign hypertrophy is comparatively rare.

JAPAN IS SPARED

Can the reason for this be isolated?

A very interesting effort to accomplish it has been made by Dr. Eiji Takahashi of Tohoku University School of Medicine in Japan. Writing in the *Tohoku Journal of Experimental Medicine* (82, 218, 1964) Dr. Takahashi reported on a very thorough statistical study he had made.

Examining the differences in nutrition between the men of Japan and the men of the United States and those of European countries with the high rate of prostatism, Dr. Takahashi found many differences, of course. The most complete of all, though, was in the kind of beverages consumed. The Japanese male consumes practically no coffee at all, drinking green tea instead. The American man is a big coffee drinker.

MEN DRINK TEA

Dr. Takahashi then went to the health statistics of the World Health Organization and the international trade statistics of the United Nations for figures. He found that in Sweden, where the age adjusted death rate for prostatic cancer is the highest in the world, this being 550 per 100,000, the coffee consumption is also the highest in the world amounting to eight kilograms per person per year.

He then went right through a list of 20 countries for the five years 1955 to 1959 and found that for nearly all of them the correlation held true--the more coffee the country consumed, the more deaths it had from prostatic cancer.

COFFEE AND CANCER

The next obvious step was to check whether any investigation had ever been made of possible cancer-causing agents in coffee. It had been done at the National Cancer Institute of the U.S. National Institutes of Health under the supervision of the famed Dr. W. C. Hueper. This study had shown that benzo-pyrene and other notorious cancer-causing hydrocarbons are present in lightly roasted and medium roasted coffees such as are consumed in the United States and in Northern Europe. Remarkably, the same types of coffee when given a very long roasting till they get extremely dark in color, as is done in Italy, no longer contain these hydrocarbons.

CARCINOGEN IN COFFEE

The Italian rate of cancer of the prostate is

about half that of the United States and less than half of the Swedish rate.

These hydrocarbons, it was further demonstrated at the National Cancer Institute, will be extracted from coffee by hot water. If they are in the ground bean, therefore, they will be in the coffee that we drink. They are present in very small amounts, so small that they might very well have no effect on a moderate drinker of coffee. But for a heavy coffee drinker, over a period of 30 or 40 years, there is good reason to suppose that this beverage can be an important cause of cancer of the prostate. And perhaps the increasing use of coffee by younger people and the fact that the coffee break two or three times a day has become a universal practice in industry, may very well account for the fact that more and more young men between the ages of 30 and 40 are contracting prostatic cancer.

COFFEE BREAKS DANGEROUS

When Dr. Takahashi attempted to make a correlation between the consumption of coffee and the death rate from cancer of any other organs than the prostate, such as the breast, uterus, stomach, intestine and rectum, he could find no correlation whatsoever. If coffee is going to cause cancer, apparently, it is going to cause it only in man and only in the prostate gland. As

ONLY PROSTATE AFFECTED

to why that should be, Dr. Takahashi has no answer and neither do I.

But even without knowing the reason, it seems a matter of simple discretion for any man to cultivate a preference for the heavily roasted black types of coffee, from which the roasting seems to remove the hydrocarbons, and to be moderate in his consumption of this delicious but dangerous beverage.

There was one other aspect of this study that could not be overlooked; and Dr. Takahashi, as a thorough and conscientious investigator, did not overlook it. It is well known that coffee consumption and sugar consumption go hand in hand. Perhaps sugar, which is also very lightly consumed in Japan, might be the reason for the high rate of prostatic cancer in the countries that are heavy consumers of coffee. This would account for the apparent discrepancy in the statistics for Austria and Hungary, both of which countries are low users of coffee but have rates of prostatic cancer nearly as high as that of the United States. These two countries are heavy users of sugar.

SUGAR ALSO SUSPECTED

Analysis of the appropriate statistics revealed that "the correlation co-efficient between sugar supply and prostate cancer mortality is as high as that between coffee and prostate cancer."

In other words, statistically it can be seen that heavy use of sugar is just as likely to cause cancer of the prostate as is heavy use of coffee.

And while no correlation could be made between coffee consumption and any other type of cancer, a definite correlation was found between sugar consumption and cancer of the breast, ovaries, intestine, and rectum.

SOME TYPES O CANCER ARE KNOWN TO BE RELATED TO SUGAR

Thus there is a distinct possibility that it is the sugar mainly in coffee, rather than the coffee itself, that is the cause of the high and ever-increasing rate of cancer of the prostate. And if so, this would neatly answer another question: Since so many men are heavy coffee users, why don't more of them get cancer of the prostate?

The answer would be that so many of them are dying of heart attacks before the cancer of the prostate has a chance to develop. Sugar, which is in a hundred ways the scourge of civilization, has been found to be a major cause of atherosclerosis and coronary attacks in men. It is also a cause of diabetes and has been implicated to some extent in lowered resistance to just about any disease you can name. You might almost say that the man who is a heavy user of sugar is lucky if he can live long enough to develop cancer of the prostate.

HEART ATTACI

Needless to say, the man who really wants to

ive out his natural span in good health, will avoid sugar in all foods, not only in coffee; and if he will also be moderate in his consumption of coffee itself, it is the opinion of Dr. Takahashi that he is no more likely than a Japanese to develop this terrible form of cancer. And that is very unlikely indeed.

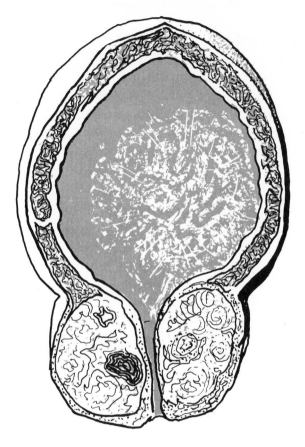

ENLARGED PROSTATE, SHOWING PRESSURE ON URETHRA

11. Sex and Your Prostate

ONE OF THE QUESTIONS that keeps arising with regard to the prostate is that of whether or not a man's sexual habits are related to what eventually happens to this sex gland. Obviously, the answer is yes. And while I wish I could say that observance of society's moral codes and standards is the best road to a healthy prostate, I am afraid that the question is not quite that simple and that when God created the prostate he was not especially considering how long it would take a young man to complete his professional education in 1966.

To consider the matter in its most basic terms, the function of the prostate gland is to manufacture the prostatic fluid. Once a sufficient amount of this fluid has been manufactured (how long this takes varies with age) the fluid should be expelled and the expulsion should be complete. That is, the prostate should be completely drained.

In general we can say that an amount of sexual activity that will permit the periodic filling and draining of the prostate, neither permitting excessive accumulations of unused fluid nor making excessive demands on the gland for the production of additional fluid, is the program that will give the prostate gland its best chance of maintaining health throughout your life.

REGULAR, WHOLESOME SEX FOR HEALTH

There is no doubt whatever that the effort to maintain regular, wholesome sex habits is going to present very special and difficult problems to the young man who cannot afford to marry or to the middle-aged widower as well as to many others. And there is nothing I can do to solve such problems, nor do I have any intention of trying. The most I can do within the scope of this work is to explore what is physiologically good for the health of the prostate and assume that every reader has a loving wife.

"Practically all of the functional disturbances of the prostate gland result from its relationship to sexual activity," says Dr. Herbert R. Kenyon in his book *The Prostate Gland.* It is a conclusion with which I would take issue, but there can be no doubt that at least some of these functional disturbances can be attributed to excessive or insufficient or improper sexual activity.

All writers on the subject remark that there is an increasing incidence of prostatic difficulties among comparatively young men in their thirties or even in their twenties. As one reads Dr. Kenyon's description of how he considers that the prostate gland is abused by young men, one can draw the conclusion that both the restrictive prohibitions of the past and the possible lack of any prohibitions that the future seems to hold in store for us, would be preferable, in terms of the health of the prostate, to the partial licence that is given our young people today. The practice of petting, by which is meant many different forms of sexual excitation without a natural conclusion, comes in for especially harsh words on the part of this doctor. He points out that prolonged engorgement (accumulation of blood such as causes an erection of the penis) extends also to the prostate and accessory glands. This constitutes a definite abuse of the glands which can be expected ultimately to lead to structural weakness.

ABUSE CAUSES DIFFICULTIES IN YOUNG MEN

PETTING IS DANGEROUS

The same, says Dr. Kenyon, is true of masturbation when carried on in the late teens or young manhood, of certain methods of birth control which do not offer complete satisfaction, such as withdrawal, and also the kind of excessive sexuality and excessive prolongation of the individual sexual act which our young people today are taught to desire through the influence Dr. Freud has had on advertising, books and indeed every area of our lives.

"Because the act is not complete," Dr. Kenyon says, "in addition to the persistent distension with blood, the violence of the muscular contractions of the prostate is diminished and the emptying of the bulb-like, secreting portions of the gland is inadequate. Consequently, the prostatic fluid is not completely discharged from some of these sacs and undergoes chemical and other changes. The products of this deterioration are irritating and often create an inflammatory response, unfavorable to the preservation of healthy tissue. A certain amount of atony (lack of strength) of the muscular portion of the prostate develops and, on subsequent ejaculation, emptying of the gland is even less complete. A vicious cycle thus forms, leading to ever-increasing functional incompetence unless it is broken by an improvement in sexual habits, proper medical therapy or both."

COMPLETE
ORGASM
IS NECESSARY

In other words, for the future of the prostate,

the best advice you can give a young man is to marry young and without a prolonged engagement.

Dr. Kenyon goes on to say that "adverse changes in the prostate gland do not result from a single unphysiologic act or cause but occur as the combination of many insults, often repeated over a considerable period of time." And he is certainly correct in this. Mistakes you made as a younger man may well have done some injury to your prostate gland, but within limits, the human body also has a considerable ability to repair injuries that it receives. It is never too late to modify your sexual attitudes and habits in order to enjoy the kind of sexual relations that will be best for your health. They will be found to be most pleasurable as well.

REPEATED INSULTS DO THE DAMAGE

The key is moderation. And what moderation means varies so greatly from one man to another, that only you, yourself, can determine what is wholesomely moderate for you.

Here are some hints to help you achieve such a determination.

FOLLOW YOUR INSTINCTS

Periodic emptying of the prostate through sexual intercourse is in every way desirable, but you should only do it when you desire it. It is only when there is a substantial accumulation of fluids produced by the prostate and other sex glands that a healthy man feels sexual desire. This can be once a week or less in a middle-aged man, or once a day or more in a very young man. In any case, it is the rate at which you produce your own secretions that will determine the desire you feel and the amount of sexual activity that is right for you.

Do not let the locker room boasts of other men or unfounded magazine articles or the misguided opinions of psychiatric writers drive you into greater sexual activity than your own system demands. The contractions of the muscle around the prostate and seminal vesicles are remarkably powerful. When they encounter sufficient fluid they are cushioned in the same way as the shock absorbers on your car cushion bumps. When there is not sufficient fluid present during an orgasm, the result may very well be hemorrhaging of the blood vessels in the delicate gland. This is an easy way to injure the gland or at the very least, to encourage infection.

AVOID EXCESS

Don't be taken in by the old wives' tale that sexual acts will decrease your strength and virility. This is true only to the extent that willingness to abstain from sex activity you do not really desire will help you to find your own natural rhythm. It is never desirable to let your

CONTINENCE IS UNDESIRABLE

glandular secretions accumulate too long, however, since they will undergo chemical de-
composition and produce products irritating and
harmful to the very gland you think you are
strengthening.

Following the above rules of thumb should
make it possible for every man to find a sexual
rhythm consistent with his age and condition of
health.

The same rules hold true if you are already
suffering from some kind of prostate trouble.
The one exception to this is the state in which
infection of the gland draws large amounts of
blood to it, leaving it engorged, which condition
can cause incredibly frequent erections of the
penis and also create a mental state of excite-
ment and sexual desire. You certainly know if
the amount of sexual excitation you feel is ab-
normally frequent and strong for you, and in
such a case would do better not to heed it in
terms of sexual activity, while giving it very
careful attention by getting examined to determine whether there is an infection.

Except in that one case, however, you will do
best to listen to the demands of your own
system, whether your prostate is in healthy
condition or otherwise. If trouble with the prostate has robbed you of all sexual desire, it is

ABNORMAL
EXCITATION
DEMANDS
INVESTIGATION

certainly something to be looked into and treated, but it would be very foolish to try to force sexual activity for which your glands are unprepared. In most cases, whatever difficulty you are having with the prostate gland will have little or no effect on your normal sexual rhythm. Discover what it is and heed it. Such wise moderation is always of some value to health.

12. The Chiropractic Treatment

C HIROPRACTIC IS A HEALING profession which, unlike the others, treats the body from the outside. It attempts to cure without resorting to either drugs or surgery, and seems to do remarkably well for large numbers of people while avoiding the risks implicit in the surgical knife and powerful drugs. The basic belief of the chiropractic profession is that most and perhaps all disease is either caused or permitted to occur because of distortions in the healthy functioning of the nervous system. In a quasi-official statement, chiropractic is explained by A. C. Johnson, D.C., as follows:

"Structural (musculo-skeletal) interferences with the nervous system, caused by falls, twists, strains, sprains, injury, body blows, distortions, faulty posture, bad occupational attitudes, living habits and other causes may affect the normal functioning of muscles, internal organs and glands in a manner peculiar to that part of the nervous system affected by the structural interference. By scientific corrective manipulation therapy the chiropractic physician corrects the structural interference which could be the cause of the disease.

"Because he specializes mostly in the nervous system, the chiropractic physician has a thorough knowledge of its functioning. Functional interferences are corrected by physical-electrotherapy means. We may activate, inhibit, stimulate, relax or accelerate the various internal organs, glands and muscles through the nervous system (according to indications), without the use of internal medicines and without harmful side effects."

When it comes to the prostate, unfortunately, while there is a drugless and bloodless treatment for both enlarged and infected prostates, not every chiropractor is familiar with it. Those who are able to apply it, though, have a good record of success in relieving or eliminating the affliction. The following discussion of the chiropractic view of the causes of prostatism and

NOT EVERY CHIROPRACTOR CAN TREAT THE PROSTATE

vhat to do about it is largely drawn from an
article by a leading chiropractor, Dr. Robert M.
Overton, which appeared in two parts in the
Journal of Chiropractic in February and March,
1965.

According to Dr. Overton, writing in the
Journal of Chiropractic in February and March,
1965, chiropractors possess two powerful
weapons in treating prostatic disorders that are
not possessed by medical doctors. First, they
understand the methods of adjusting the
pressures of the skeleton in order to relieve the
nerves of strains and pressures that prevent
their proper functioning. And secondly, not
believing in surgical intervention except as a
last resort, chiropractors are more willing to try
natural means of correcting the disorder.

ORIENTED
TOWARD
NATURAL
TREATMENT

Dr. Overton lists the following chiropractic
techniques as being useful and helpful in the
treatment of prostatitis, while cautioning that
overnight results cannot be expected but that
from 20 to 50 treatments over a period of several
months are necessary to bring about relief or
cure:

1. "Diathermy is indicated in practically all
diseases of the prostate gland," he states. This
is a procedure by which a high frequency (or
short wave) current is passed through the body,

DIATHERMY

inducing an internal rise in temperature in the deep tissues. One device that chiropractors possess is a mechanism built right into the chair on which the patient sits. Sitting in the chair for about 15 minutes increases the temperature in and around the prostate gland and thus acts like a localized fever to combat infection. Some chiropractors will immediately follow this treatment with treatment by an ultrasound mechanism that subjects the prostate to sound waves above the range of hearing of the human ear, a type of therapy that has also been found to have a health-giving and infection-relieving effect. Dr. Overton points out that ultrasound therapy "is always greater in effect when preceded by diathermy."

ULTRASOUND

2. For the same reason that diathermy is used, which is primarily that fever is the body's own natural way of destroying infection, the chiropractic profession recommends that prostatitis be treated by fever therapy if the chiropractor has the equipment. It is complicated and expensive equipment and not every chiropractor will have it. What it does is to give the patient an artificial, sometimes localized fever of 102 to 103 degrees, which is maintained for an hour at a time. The treatment is given every two or three days and it is Dr. Overton's claim that "these

FEVER THERAPY

cases will generally clear up faster than with any other type of therapy."

3. High on Dr. Overton's list of ways the chiropractor can help the prostate patient is the subject of diet. Pointing out that over a long period of time, vitamins are practically useless unless they are accompanied in the diet by a full range of mineral nutrients, he recommends that the chiropractor dispense a natural calcium or mineral formula, such as bone meal, to reinforce and make more effective the helpful vitamin and mineral supplements.

VITAMINS A AND C

Vitamin A is recommended in the amount of 75,000 international units daily for 30 days, being reduced after that to 50,000 international units daily. The prostate has been found to have an affinity to vitamin A (and I would add vitamin C) that would lead any health-minded individual to deduce that these vitamins must be connected with prostatic health. Indeed, both these vitamins are intimately connected with the ability of the soft tissues and mucous membranes to fight off infections anywhere in the body. And that is probably why they both have been found to concentrate in the prostate gland which is so vulnerable to infection in middle age.

For those who show a premature slowing down of the sexual urge (prior to the age of 50) in conjunction with a prostatic involvement, from 500 to 800 milligrams a day of natural vitamin E is recommended. This vitamin has been shown to be essential to the reproductive system and is an obvious nutritional measure to counter any unnatural weakness of that system.

VITAMIN E

And as a final note on the chiropractic recommendations for nutritional measures against prostatism, where the case is diagnosed as simple benign enlargement of the prostate, a natural vitamin F complex (unrefined, cold-pressed vegetable oil such as soy, wheat germ or corn) is recommended to be added to the above regimen. This, according to Dr. Overton, "causes marked reduction in size, disappearance of part or all of the pain and discomfort. Nocturia is eliminated in 68 per cent of the tested cases and it also causes an increase in sexual libido."

To these important dietary measures, the chiropractors also add a general recommendation that has been found valuable in many cases. It is to eliminate from the diet those foods that leave residual acid in the system and thus cause an excessively acid condition of the blood. The list includes some foods that are valuable in the normal diet and should not be eliminated except for medical reasons. For the sufferer from prostatism, however, it would certainly be worth-

ELIMINATE
ACID RESIDUES

while to experiment with eliminating all the following foods from the diet to see if this does not bring relief. Here are the foods to avoid: dried lima beans, navy beans, peas, lentils, asparagus, pumpkin, winter squash, plums, prunes, cranberries, rhubarb, coffee, tea, all forms of alcohol, all spices and condiments, pickles, ketchup, horseradish, shellfish, all poultry, and gravies.

FOODS TO AVOID

4. When it comes to spinal adjustment, which is the primary therapy of chiropractic, the general opinion is that even though prostatism is not caused by displacement of the vertebrae, adjustments nevertheless play a role in its therapy. Manual concussion, which is a technical term for a blow with the fist, when applied to certain of the lowest vertebrae in the spinal column is said to stimulate the sacral nerves and temporarily reduce the size of an enlarged prostate. There are other chiropractic procedures to adjust the position of any of the low back vertebrae that may be more or less displaced and to eliminate such interfering conditions as spasticity of the muscles of the rectal wall. It is believed that all these corrections play a role in permitting maximum effectiveness of such other therapies as may be used. In addition, the stimulation of the sacral nerves is considered

SPINAL ADJUSTMENT

obligatory whether they themselves show any need for it or not, because of the effect this has on the size of the prostate and because the passage of urine can be encouraged in this way.

5. In conjunction with spinal adjustments and concussion, many chiropractors feel that a sitz bath at home is of definite benefit. It is recom- SITZ BATH
mended that such a bath be taken daily for ten to fifteen minutes. The patient sits in the tub with his legs pulled up against his chest and with only enough water in the tub to cover the hips and buttocks. The tub temperature should be 100 degrees Fahrenheit when the patient enters it and should then be increased from six to 15 degrees, depending on what is found comfortable.

The warmth draws blood to the region which is always a help when the problem is to fight against a localized infection.

6. Lastly, the chiropractor will sometimes use the technique of prostate massage, which he considers not massage at all but rather manipu- PROSTATE MASSAGE
lation of the prostate gland to remove the possibly infected secretions it contains. This is similar in its objective to such a technique as lancing a boil. It does not pretend or aim to do anything about the cause of an existing infection, but simply relieves pain and tension

and makes it somewhat more possible for the body to fight against an infection with its own resources by the removal of a good proportion of accumulated pus and other infection-containing fluids.

Prostatic massage is performed with a gloved hand, a finger being inserted into the rectum so that it can apply a gentle pressure directly against the prostate. It should not be done more than once in two weeks because of the danger of irritating the delicate gland. If there is any possibility whatsoever of carcinoma of the prostate, it should not be done at all.

How reliable is the chiropractic treatment for prostatitis? Can one expect sure relief? Can one expect a cure?

The answers to these questions depend almost entirely on the skill of the individual chiropractor who is treating you. Therefore, there is no such thing as a reliable statistic on what proportion of chiropractic treatments are successful. One chiropractor will claim, and probably truthfully and accurately, that he is almost uniformly successful in reducing or eliminating prostatic hypertrophies. Another will have much more limited success or none at all. It is certainly advisable, if you go in for chiropractic treatment at all, to try to find a

SKILL IS
REQUIRED

practitioner who has long and successful experience with this particular affliction. Given such an experienced and skillful doctor, the chances are very good that he can at least benefit the condition to an appreciable extent. It is probably worth taking the chance, since in any case he will not do you any harm. I, myself, if I were having trouble with my prostate, would certainly go to a doctor of chiropractic before even thinking of surgery.

There are certain types of prostatitis that a chiropractor should not attempt to treat at all. They are those that stem from a gonorrheal infection, or those involving carcinoma, tuberculosis, or an abscess, and most common, those in which the urethra has already been closed, which necessitates immediate surgical intervention.

MEDICAL PROBLEMS OUT OF CHIROPRACTIC SPHERE

There is no reason to suppose that any ethical doctor of chiropractic would attempt to treat such types of prostatism or would be unaware of them and thus delay necessary medical treatments. The diagnostic techniques of the skilled chiropractor should certainly be adequate to detect any of these conditions. When they are detected, the chiropractor will not attempt to treat them but will refer them to a medical doctor.

13. When To Have an Operation

I F YOU BELIEVE THAT you have prostate trouble or suspect that it may be developing, this will probably be because you are having difficulties with urination. Dribbling and difficulty in completely emptying the bladder in almost 100% of cases are the signs that first bring a man to the doctor, who will then diagnose whether or not there is prostatic hypertrophy (enlargement). If you even suspect prostatitis, you should definitely go to the doctor for diagnosis. The reason: "Prostatic cancer is the most common malignant neoplasm in men in this country with the possible exception of skin cancer." That is the statement of Reubin H. Flocks, M. D., Urologist of the University of Iowa

College of Medicine and Hospital. It is undoubt-
edly an accurate evaluation of the cancer hazard
that is involved potentially in difficulties with
the prostate. Since there is such a distinct
hazard, it would be the height of unwisdom, on
noticing the beginning of prostatic trouble in
yourself, to fail to consult your physician for a
thorough diagnosis.

MEDICAL
EXAMINATION
INDISPENSABLE

And if he should find a malignancy already
developed, he will recommend surgery and you
should go along with his recommendation. The
operation for the removal of the prostate is a
serious one. It is not to be entered into lightly.
But it is practically never fatal, and when it is a
question of saving your life, such surgery is
certainly justified. It has succeeded in saving
the lives of many thousands of men. Caught
early enough, the malignancy can usually be
removed entirely without metastases--loose
cancer cells that spread through the blood
stream.

I do believe that a cancerous prostate gland
should be removed. I also believe that a
confirmed diagnosis of cancer is just about the
only reason a man should ever have an operation
on his prostate, unless he has already tried
every other measure and secured no relief.

CANCER
REQUIRES
SURGERY

We have already referred to the pioneering

work of Dr. Sieve who proved that good nutrition will bring better results than surgery when hypertrophy of the prostate is not malignant. Because this work is so appropriate to a discussion of when to have an operation and when to avoid one, let us review it here.

In an article in *The American Journal of Digestive Diseases*, December, 1951, Dr. Sieve described his experience with 100 cases of prostatic trouble and regarding them he said, "In 70 per cent, the operative stage was prevented." Besides using some medication, and massage, he depended a great deal on the use of vitamins A, B, C, D, and E, and gave his patients a food supplement in capsule form made from alfalfa, buckwheat and soybean. He found in practically all cases an upset in the nutritional balance of these people; that they were nutritional cripples so to speak, and yet most of them were eating what are considered good diets.

OPERATIONS CAN BE AVOIDED

Basically, malnutrition is at the bottom of most diseases and Dr. Sieve describes individual cases where men were suffering from prostate disease but when their malnutrition was cured, not only were they relieved of their prostatic symptoms, but they lost their constipation, headaches and many other conditions, and could sleep much better. In one case the patient, after treatment, looked twenty years younger. So the method we are describing holds terrific possibilities for the health of people in general.

Dr. Sieve says that 55 per cent of all men who reach the age of sixty will develop some kind of prostatic trouble. In other words, more than one out of every two men who reach sixty will have prostatic disease in some form or other, so you can see how important it is, as a preventive measure, to follow healthful nutritional habits.

NUTRITION IS THE GREAT PROTECTOR

Dr. Sieve is not the only medical man who has spoken out against needless prostatic surgery. Dr. T. L. Chapman, urological surgeon of the Victoria Infirmary in Glasgow, Scotland, wrote about it in *The Lancet,* a British medical journal, in the October 15, 1949 issue. He said, "Some surgeons perform prostatectomy on all patients referred to them with prostatic enlargement and urinary symptoms, their aim being to eliminate so far as possible the advanced 'bad risk' case." But why should the mild case pay for the advanced bad risk case? The doctor adds, "It is certainly unjustifiable to remove the prostate merely because it is enlarged and has been associated with some urinary symptoms." This is an age of specialization. Many of these physicians, especially surgeons, do not study or deal with nutrition because it is outside of their specialty, and they are, therefore, not aware of the part that corrective nutrition could play in prostatic disease.

Incidentally, Dr. Chapman, in his article, shows that out of 129 cases of prostatic trouble that he treated, only seventeen needed an operation, which is only about 15 per cent.

DOCTORS CRITICIZE EXCESSIVE SURGERY

Dr. Theron Clagett, M.D., a Mayo Clinic surgeon, says, "We are in a terrible trend, toward too fast and too radical surgery."

Here is a statement made by the editor of the *Medical Press* of London, in an editorial in the March 13, 1957 issue. "There are many patients with some prostatic symptoms in whom operation is not only unnecessary but may be useless or even harmful."

Dr. George C. Prather, president of the American Urological Association gave a presidential address that was reported in *The Journal of Urology*, issue of August, 1956, in which he said, "Patients should not be operated upon just because they have an enlarged prostate, a few obstructive symptoms and very little or no residual urine."

In his speech he described a question that was put to a certain group of surgeons. The question was: If the patient has no urinary infection, no inflammation of the prostate gland, but a residue of urine of sixty cc or less, would it be advisable to operate? Sixty per cent of the surgeons said "yes" and 40 per cent said "no." The condition Dr. Prather described is the mildest of the mild types of prostatic trouble, ninety per cent of which could easily yield to treatment, yet sixty per cent of reputable surgeons advised surgery.

We don't want anyone to think that we are not in favor of operating on the prostate when it is absolutely necessary. If the disease has progressed beyond a certain point, then it is too late to expect diet, etc., to be of much help. What we are trying to stress is that a man should begin early to prevent it by good diet and exercise.

Judging by my own results, the *Prevention* system which I have worked out over a period of twenty years must be a perfect preventive of prostate difficulties. I am 68 years old and have not been bothered a single day by any prostate symptoms. I attribute this to the fact that my diet already includes large amounts of pumpkin and sunflower seeds plus very substantial supplements of all the vitamins and minerals. With the recent addition of high-magnesium dolomite tablets to my regime, I believe I have secured for myself the final insurance against prostatitis.

PERSONAL DISCIPLINE WORKS

But if I were being bothered--if I were starting to find that I had to get up once or twice in the middle of the night to urinate or if I were dribbling urine now and then, I would immedi- ately refer to the preceding chapters of this book and resort, without exception, to every single dietary measure that it mentions. There is not one of them that can do any harm. There is no point that I can see in experimenting with one- self and trying first one and then the other, to see which is going to do the most good. Every one of them has been proven to be of some definite value in this affliction. Why not use them all?

DIETARY MEASURES CAN DO NO HARM

If you do, you can be sure that you are taking advantage of every natural means ever dis- covered to keep your prostate in good health or get it that way.

In addition, I would exercise moderately, not straining myself but making certain that my blood was circulating vigorously and I was not losing any muscle tone through inactivity. I would make sure of getting enough rest and if I were overweight, I would embark on a program of gradual weight loss. Above all, I would def- initely eliminate any health-destructive vices I might have, such as smoking or drinking or using coffee or sugar.

EXERCISE HELPS

This advice is advice that spells general good health and the best possible resistance to sickness of any kind. It could hardly help being of definite value to the prostate gland as well as to all the rest of the human system.

Only if I had tried all these measures, not for a few days but for at least six months, and then found that my prostate condition was getting worse instead of getting better, would I be willing to consider surgery.

No, I'm not against surgery. I simply consider it a last resort that should practically never be necessary to a man without cancer who has read this book intelligently.

Index

The text of this book is set in 11 point Uranus, a modern photo type that is finding increasing favor in scientific publishing for its combination of simplicity and non-fatiguing readability. The marginal notes are the same type, Uranus, in 8 point capitals. Chapter headings are 24 point Garamond. The book was manufactured by Sowers Printing Company, Lebanon, Pennsylvania. It was edited and designed by Harald J. Taub.